The best

Scented Plants

By

ROGER PHILLIPS
& MARTYN RIX

50p

Research by Alison Rix
Design Jill Bryan & Debby Curry

A Pan Original

Acknowledgements

We would like to thank the following gardens and
suppliers for allowing us to visit them and
photograph their plants:
The Royal Horticultural Society's Garden, Wisley;
the Royal Botanic Gardens, Kew; the University
Botanic Garden, Cambridge; the Savill garden,
Windsor; Eccleston Square Gardens; The Lost
Gardens of Heligan, Cornwall; Arley Hall, Cheshire;
Gravetye Manor, Sussex; Cranbourne Manor,
Dorset; Knightshayes, Devon; Hever Castle, Kent;
Powis Castle; the Old Vicarage, Edington; Spetchley
Park, Worcestershire; Littlewood Park, Scotland; the
gardens at Ninfa, Italy; Monet's garden at Giverny;
Serre de la Madonne; David Austin's Nursery and
Goatchers' Arboretum, Sussex.

Among others who have helped in one way or another
we would like to thank: John d'Arcy, Clair Austin,
Odile Mesqualier and Marilyn Inglis.

First published 1998 by Pan
an imprint of Macmillan Publishers Limited
25 Eccleston Place, London SW1W 9NF
and Basingstoke
Associated companies throughout the world
ISBN 0-330-35550-3
Copyright in the text and illustrations
© Roger Phillips and Martyn Rix
The right of the authors to be identified as the
authors of this work has been asserted by them in
accordance with the Copyright, Designs and
Patents Act 1988.
9 8 7 6 5 4 3 2 1
A CIP catalogue record for this book is available
from the British Library

Colour Reproduction by Aylesbury Studios Ltd.
Printed by Butler and Tanner Ltd. Frome, Somerset

Contents

Nepeta and lavender, contrasted with clumps of irises at Gravetye Manor, Sussex

Introduction

Plants are valued for many things – among the most important are colour, form and scent, and it is to the last that this book is devoted. Scent adds an extra dimension to the garden, bringing with it pleasure, memories and associations; the aromatic smell of herbs reminds us of the kitchen; roses, lily-of-the-valley and rose-geranium conjure up fragrant baths, while honeysuckle brings to mind the pervasive, slightly peppery smell of a summer country walk between hedges smothered with wild honeysuckle.

For the plants themselves, of course, scent is a more serious business, as it is an important attractant for pollinating insects. In many species, the pale or insignificantly coloured flowers are the most fragrant; brightly coloured petals, especially red ones, attract by sight and do not need to waste

Daphne odora

energy on scent as well. Good examples of this can be seen in the cultivated freesias, where only the yellow or white varieties smell strongly, or in honeysuckles, where the bird-pollinated, red-flowered *Lonicera sempervirens* from North America is scentless.

English roses and ramblers at David Austin's Nursery, near Wolverhampton

Loss of scent often occurs in those plants which have been bred specifically for other purposes. Many florists' roses or Hybrid Teas, which are selected for their strong stems and length of flowering have very little scent; on the other hand, most of the 'old roses' have a wonderful scent. So if you particularly wish to obtain scented plants, you will need to know the exact name of the species or variety. Although there are groups of plants in which all the members will be scented, some are usually superior to others, and others may have no scent at all.

Dianthus 'Marg's Choice', a modern pink

How to use this book

We have arranged the plants in roughly chronological flowering order, starting with spring and working through the seasons, based on the normal flowering time in the cooler parts of the Northern Hemisphere. Within this framework, we have, where possible, grouped the plants more or less in families, selecting a few of the best from each group.

The majority of plants are hardy, but we have included a few more tender plants, which require greenhouse or other protection in northern Europe and eastern North America, but which can be grown outside in warmer climates. An approximate guide to hardiness is given for each plant, but the natural world is flexible, so if you are prepared to try plants at the limits of their hardiness, you may be lucky (and surprised).

Choosing plants

Before you decide which plants you would like to grow, have a careful think about your garden, its climate and soil, and start by selecting those plants that like similar conditions. For instance, lavenders will do well in well-drained soil on a sunny slope and will be miserable in a cold clay soil. Roses, on the other hand, do best in heavy clay soils and are miserable in light, sandy soil.

Philadelphus 'Avalanche'

Where to obtain plants

Start by visiting your local nursery. There are numerous small nurseries which are very good sources of plants and will know which plants thrive in your area. Where possible, choose young, actively growing plants, not those which have been sitting in their pots for months. Try to buy plants sold from the open ground or those grown in soil, as they will do better in the open garden than those grown in peat-based compost. Plants are grown in peat compost for the convenience of the grower, not the customer.

If you have time, visit gardens open to the public and make notes of plants you like. You can then buy them locally or purchase them by mail order. Sources for the rarer plants can be found by looking in the following:

The RHS Plant Finder devised by Chris Philip is published annually. It gives details of nurseries and the whole range of plants stocked in Britain. It is invaluable when searching for specific plants, but you will need to look under the Latin name (given in brackets next to the common name in this book). Obtainable in bookshops.
The Andersen Horticultural Library's Source List of Plants & Seeds is the American equivalent of *The Plant Finder*. Obtainable from A. H. L., Minnesota Landscape Arboretum, 3675 Arboretum Drive, PO Box 39, Chanhassen, MN 55317-0039, USA.
PPP Index is the European *Plant Finder*, published both as a book and as a CDRom in German, French and English by Eugen Ulmer GmbH, Wollgrasweg 41, 70599 Stuttgart.

Growing & siting plants

As with all plants, success in growing scented plants comes from providing conditions as near as possible to their natural habitat (*see above*). The only thing that should be borne in mind specifically when growing scented or aromatic plants is that they should be placed where the smell can be enjoyed by humans as well as insects. For

Lilac 'Maud Notcutt'

Night-scented stock *Matthiola longipetala* subsp. *bicornis*; the flowers open on a dull day

Spanish Broom *Spartium junceum*

aromatic plants, those with foliage which has to be brushed against or crushed before the smell is released, a raised situation near a door, archway, path or outdoor dining area makes sense, while for the creepers, such as pennyroyal, a crack in the path will do.

The same applies to small plants with an airborne scent, such as night-scented stock, but for larger shrubs with a strong scent that floats on the air, such as *Philadelphus*, there is more leeway, although it would be a pity for the scent to be wasted, which will happen if the plant is too far from the normal routes round your garden. Climbing scented plants, such as roses and honeysuckle, can be grown around doors and windows, or over pergolas, arches and bowers so that the scent may be enjoyed when sitting or walking nearby. Lastly, do not forget those flowers, such as freesias or pinks, which can be cut and brought into the house, releasing their scent indoors.

A climbing honeysuckle *Lonicera caprifolium*

Wintersweet *Chimonanthus praecox* in the winter garden at the University Botanic Garden, Cambridge

Winter-flowering Shrubs

The small number of plants which flower at the beginning of the year are particularly valuable. Although these flowers are generally small as they have to survive the rigours of winter, they often have good scent which is carried on the air in order to attract early pollinators. Shrubs can be planted at any time from autumn to spring. Wherever possible, buy plants which have been grown locally in the open ground, as they will do much better in the long run. When planting pot-grown shrubs, carefully remove as much of the old compost as possible and replant in fresh soil in a suitable site.

Corylopsis

Corylopsis sinensis var. ***willmottiae*** A deciduous shrub that grows to about 12ft (3.5m) tall, with hanging clusters of small yellow flowers

in spring. Native to China. Hardy to 0°F (−18°C), US zones 7–10.

Forma ***veitchiana*** (*Not illustrated*) This makes a smaller bush, up to about 8ft (2.5m) tall, with shorter racemes of flowers with red stamens.

PLANTING HELP Corylopsis likes a warm, slightly shady position, in moist, leafy soil and protection from spring frosts. No pruning needed.

Wintersweet

Chimonanthus praecox A spreading deciduous shrub that grows to 10ft (3m) across. This rather insignificant-looking shrub should be given a place on the house wall, as the more heat it

Corylopsis sinensis var. *willmottiae*

Hamamelis mollis with Rhododendrons   *Viburnum × bodnantense* 'Dawn'

absorbs in the summer the better it will flower in the winter, usually between December and February. The flowers are small, cream and spiky, with a superb spicy scent, born on the previous year's wood. Native to China, where it grows in the mountains of Hubei and Sichuan. For best results prune lightly immediately after flowering. Hardy to −20°F (−29°C), US zones 5–9.

PLANTING HELP   Make sure it is well watered during the growing period. A good dressing of manure or compost will aid healthy growth.

Hamamelis × intermedia 'Jelena'

Witch-hazel

Witch-hazels or *Hamamelis* are elegant deciduous shrubs or small trees, related to *Corylopsis*. They have sharply scented small flowers about 1in (2.5cm) across, formed of 4 unusual strap-shaped yellow to red petals and short purplish sepals. There are many different species and forms available: the earliest-flowering and most fragrant is *Hamamelis mollis*, which bears golden yellow flowers from December to February; 'Jelena' is a good variety of *Hamamelis × intermedia* with

orange flowers; 'Pallida', a variety of *Hamamelis mollis* has pale yellow flowers. The hazel-like leaves appear in late spring after the flowers have faded. Very hardy, down to −10°F (−23°C), US zones 6–9.

PLANTING HELP   In the wild *Hamamelis* usually grow in scrub and woods, so they do best in partial shade and in leafy soil.

Hamamelis mollis 'Pallida'

Viburnums

One of the very best groups of shrubs with regard to scent. Although the later-flowering species are shown on page 28, there are two species which flower much earlier in the year than the others, so we have included a hybrid between them in this section.

Viburnum × bodnantense **'Dawn'**   A hybrid between *Viburnum farreri* (very good for scent) and *V. grandiflorum*, with some of the best features of both parents. It is a deciduous shrub that eventually grows to 10ft (3m) high, bearing whitish pink flowers in autumn and winter and deeper pink flowers in the spring. Hardy to −10°F (−23°C), US zones 6–9.

PLANTING HELP   Easy to grow in almost any soil in sun or shade.

Hyacinths planted in gravel in a bowl in the cold greenhouse; ten bulbs together make a fine display

Iris

Iris reticulata An attractive dwarf bulbous iris that grows to 6in (15cm) tall, with deep purple, violet-scented flowers in early spring. The dark blue purple variety smells best; those hybrids with larger paler flowers are crosses with the scentless *Iris histrioides*. Native to northern Turkey and Iran. Hardy to 0°F (–18°C), US zones 7–10.

PLANTING HELP   Plant the bulbs in autumn in a pot of sandy soil and leave outside in a cold place until early spring when the buds appear. After flowering put the plants into the open garden immediately, where, if you are lucky, they may establish and flower in later years.

Hyacinths

Some of the best-known of the early-flowering bulbs, hyacinths can be grown successfully in the garden, and are much appreciated when brought inside as pot plants, as the heavy scent of just two or three bulbs can fill a small room. There are countless forms and varieties of hyacinths available, many of which have been 'prepared' for growing as pot plants, and there are also types which can be grown outside. The wild *Hyacinthus orientalis* is native to Turkey, Syria and the Lebanon, where it grows in dry rocky places, so it is best grown in the garden in well-drained sandy soil in full sun. If kept rather dry during the summer, it should flourish and produce flowers from February to May. Most people, however, will be more familiar with the larger-flowered sorts, such as those shown here.

PLANTING HELP   For indoor flowering, groups of specially prepared bulbs should be planted during early autumn in bowls of moist bulb fibre, a special type of open peaty compost. Keep the bulbs moist, as cool as possible (below 50°F (10°C), and in the dark, until the flower buds are clear of the leaves, usually around mid-winter. Then bring the bowls into the warmth and light to flower. Planted in the open ground, unprepared bulbs will flower in spring. Hardy to 0°F (–18°C), US zones 7–10.

Grape Hyacinth

Grape Hyacinths flower later than the large hyacinths and have a characteristic sweet, sharp scent in their tiny rounded flowers.

Muscari armeniacum and **M. neglectum**
Two of the commonest species in cultivation; both have stems that are around 6in (15cm) tall and leaves that flop on the ground. The flowers of *M. armeniacum* are mid-blue, around ¼in (0.5cm) long in a short head. *M. neglectum* has flowers which are usually dark Prussian blue, with white teeth at the mouth, often slightly larger, and with the best scent. Both are easy to grow in any good garden soil and will increase well. Hardy to −10°F (−23°C), US zones 6–9.

Muscari macrocarpum This species and its relative *M. muscarimi*, the original musk hyacinth grown by the Turks and Greeks before the 16th century, are the best for scent. The greenish yellow flowers of *M. macrocarpum* are around ½in (1.5cm) long, in a lax spike to 1ft (30cm) tall. Hardy to 0°F (−18°C), US zones 7–10.

PLANTING HELP   If grown in a pot, musk hyacinths can be brought into the house when in flower, where their scent will fill the air. They need well-drained limy soil.

Close-up of white hyacinth

Mixed *Iris reticulata*, with the dark blue purple variety in the centre

Muscari neglectum

Muscari macrocarpum from cliffs on the island of Kos

Wild Primrose *Primula vulgaris*

Primrose

Primrose *Primula vulgaris*   The most characteristic early spring flowers of woods and hedgebanks in England. The rosettes of puckered leaves surround the dense mass of yellow flowers on stems 4–8in (10–20cm) long. Flowers of other colours are found in southern Europe; pink ones are common in Greece and Turkey, white in the Balearic Islands. Their sweet, uncloying scent is shared by several other spring flowers. Hardy to −30°F (−35°C), US zones 4–8.

PLANTING HELP   Primroses are easy to grow provided they have shade in summer. They prefer a heavy, humus-rich soil which is not too acid and they grow well on chalk.

Sweet Violets

Viola odorata   These small flowers have a sweet scent which can be detected at a distance on a warm spring day, particularly by men; women seem to detect this scent less readily. Wild violets are usually deep purple or white, and are commonest on hedgebanks on chalky and clay soils. Garden varieties are known in pink, apricot and pale yellow as well. Hardy to −30°F (−35°C), US zones 4–8.
'Alba'   A pure white form.
'Governor Herrick'   A fine garden violet with large, deep purple flowers around 1¼in (3cm) across. A hybrid, possibly with the American wild species *Viola sororia*.

PLANTING HELP   All violets are easily grown, provided they have some shade in summer, and do better if they are replanted every other year. Most form runners, or seed in summer.

Phlox

Crawling Phlox *Phlox stolonifera*   This flower is to the woodlands of the Applachians what primroses are to English woods, one of the favourite flowers of spring. Delicately scented, pale blue, purple or pink flowers, about 10 in a loose head on a stem that may grow to 10in (25cm) tall, though usually around half this high, between April and June. The cultivar 'Blue Ridge' has flowers of a good pale blue. Very hardy to −30°F (−35°C), US zones 4–8.

PLANTING HELP   The plant spreads by runners to form loose mats, and these can be detached to make new plants. Best in a warm position, under light shade, in stony, leafy soil, with water in summer.

Crawling Phlox *Phlox stolonifera*

Hybrid violet 'Governor Herrick'

Viola odorata 'Alba'

Winter Heliotrope

Petasites fragrans Victorian gardeners were responsible for the introduction of many noxious weeds as garden plants; this is one of them, and the even larger Japanese *Petasites* and Japanese Knotweed *Polygonum cuspidatum* are others. They were fine for the wild gardens of huge country houses, but being almost ineradicable, are a pest in today's small plots. They also have a tendency to escape and invade hedges where they overwhelm the native plants. Winter Heliotrope's redeeming feature is the lovely sweet scent of its greyish flowers which may appear as early as November .

A cold winter kills the round leaves, but the roots survive. Native to Italy, Sicily and North Africa. Hardy only to 10°F (−12°C), US zones 8–10.

PLANTING HELP
Put this only in a safe place on the edge of the garden or in a large pot, from which its underground rhizomes will be unable to escape. It thrives in deep, heavy and moist soil.

Winter Heliotrope *Petasites fragrans*

Winter Heliotrope

Prunus mume 'Benichidori' and 'Omoinomama'

Jasminum polyanthum on a rusticated arbor

Japanese Apricot

Prunus mume   One of the loveliest of early-flowering shrubs, long cultivated in China and Japan. In the wild in SW China it forms a small tree, but in gardens is usually a shrub to 10ft (3m), recognized by its long green twigs and deep pink or white, single or double flowers, with a delicate scent which hangs in the air on warm, early spring days. Several old cultivars have been introduced from Japan: 'Ominato' has large, single, mid-pink flowers around 1in (2.5cm) across; in 'Benichidori', perhaps the most elegant, the flowers are deep pink and slightly smaller; in 'Omoinomama' the flowers are semi-double and vary from pink to white on the same branch. In 'Pendula' the branches weep, the flowers are pale pink. Hardy to –10°F (–23°C), US zones 6–9.

PLANTING HELP   Easily grown in woodland conditions, needing a warm summer to set good buds. The early leaves may be affected by Peach Leaf Curl, but soon grow out of it.

Jasmine

Jasminum polyanthum   A Chinese climber that grows to 20ft (6m) or more, with white flowers from pink buds produced in profusion in late winter and spring. This plant is forced in huge numbers to flower in winter in pots, but is then a sad shadow of its true self. It can, under ideal conditions, cover a sunny wall or arbor with powerfully scented flowers. Hardy to 20°F (–6°C), US zones 9–10.

PLANTING HELP   Any good soil will suit this species, which needs water in summer until it is established. It must have full sun to flower well, even in California.

Abeliophyllum

Abeliophyllum distichum
An attractive early-flowering shrub that grows to around 6ft (2m) and is like a dwarf scented Forsythia, with pink buds that usually open to white flowers around 4¼in (11cm) long. It is wild in Korea and does very well on the east coast of North America. Very hardy to –20°F (–29°C), US zones 5–9.

PLANTING HELP   Needs a warm wall in mild areas such as England, but is good as a free-standing bush in warmer climates, as it needs summer heat to set its flower buds. Prune in early summer, cutting out the shoots which have flowered, while the new leafy shoots are encouraged and trained. Any good soil.

Abeliophyllum distichum

Osmanthus delavayi at the Royal Botanic Gardens, Kew

Osmanthus × burkwoodii

Osmanthus

Osmanthus are mostly evergreen shrubs from Asia, which have small flowers but are famous for their scent. The most highly prized is *Osmanthus fragrans (not shown)*, a tender species from S China, with small, insignificant flowers, usually white but also orange or yellowish green, and produced from September to November. It is rather tender, but good in Florida, California and the Mediterranean area. Hardy to 20°F (−6°C), US zones 9–10. The other species shown here are hardy useful shrubs with small, scented, white flowers. Some are superficially very like holly, but may be recognized easily by their opposite, not alternate leaves.

PLANTING HELP   All Osmanthus tolerate chalky soils; they should be planted in autumn in mild areas or in late spring in sun or partial shade, and watered in dry summers.

Osmanthus delavayi   While most Osmanthus are renowned for their scent, *O. delavayi* has lovely flowers shaped like small white trumpets which can cover the whole shrub in spring. The plant is evergreen with dark green, stiff leaves to 1in (2.5cm) long; the shrub can eventually make 20ft (6m). This is one of the best small shrubs for the garden, thriving on acid or chalky soils. Hardy down to 0°F (−18°C), US zones 7–10.

Osmanthus × burkwoodii   A hybrid designed to combine the large flowers of *O. delavayi* with the greater hardiness of *O. decorus*, a native to the south Caucasus and northeast Turkey. The result is a neat shrub with evergreen entire leaves and masses of small white flowers. It is an easy but slow-growing shrub, finally reaching 10ft (3m). Hardy to −10°F (−23°C), US zones 6–9.

Osmanthus heterophyllus   The most holly-like species, and like holly, the leaves are sometimes lobed and slightly spiny, sometimes entire. The flowers are small and white, usually produced in autumn and winter. It is a native to Japan, as far north as south Honshu. Hardy to −10°F (−23°C), US zones 6–9.

Osmanthus
heterophyllus

Narcissus

Narcissus are typical flowers of late spring; the earliest daffodils such as 'February Gold' may open in late February or March, while the latest, the Late Pheasant Eye *Narcissus poeticus* var. *recurvus* may still be in flower in early June in Scotland, Maine or Canada. The strongest scented are the jonquils, with small bright yellow flowers; these and their hybrids have been famous for their scent since the 16th century. Slightly less powerful are the Tazetta type and the Paper Whites which can be forced to flower indoors in mid-winter. The Pheasant Eyes are very sweet and slightly less pungent than the Tazettas. Finally, the common yellow daffodils, though still scented, are the most delicate of all.

PLANTING HELP   Daffodil bulbs are usually bought in autumn and should be planted as soon as possible, in good soil. It is even better to get them from a friend and move them 'in the green', as soon as they have flowered. Prepared bulbs of Paper Whites should be planted as early as possible and will thrive in a bowl of wet gravel.

'Soleil d'Or' *Narcissus tazetta* subsp. *aureus* Similar to Paper White, but with yellow flowers and a heavier scent. Will do well outside in a warm position. Also good for forcing. Hardier than Paper White, to 10°F (−12°C), US zones 8–10.

Jonquil *Narcissus jonquilla*

Paper White *Narcissus papyraceus*   Robust bulbs with leaves and flowers appearing in winter and spring. The stems grow to 2ft (60cm) and the flowers are pure white. Needs good soil with ample water in winter and warmth in summer. Good for forcing indoors, but difficult to flower a second time. Grows well outdoors in California and around the Mediterranean where it is wild. Not very hardy to 20°F (−6°C), US zones 9–10.

Jonquil *Narcissus jonquilla*   These wild jonquils have small, bright yellow flowers around 1in (2.5cm) across, in groups of 2–5, on a stem that grows to 9in (23cm), with dark green, rush-like foliage. Easily grown in a sunny position, moist in winter, dry in summer. Long grown in the gardens of northern Europe for their sweet, intense scent. Hardy to 10°F (−12°C), US zones 8–10.

***Narcissus* 'Trevithian'**   A jonquil hybrid with excellent scent good for growing outdoors or in a pot, with narrow, dark green leaves and bright yellow flowers of good substance. Hardy to 10°F (−12°C), US zones 8–10.

Pheasant Eye *Narcissus poeticus*   The common *N. poeticus* has graceful stems and flowers with white petals and a very small green and red corona; it flowers at about the same time as daffodils and has a lovely, sharp but delicate scent. Best in moist soil or planted in rough grass. Var. *recurvus* flowers later and has stiffer, recurved petals. Hardy to −30°F (−35°C), US zones 4–8.

'Soleil d'Or'

A clump of Pheasant Eye *Narcissus poeticus* in Devon in April

Narcissus 'Trevithian'

Paper Whites *Narcissus papyraceus*

Daphnes

Daphnes are neat and usually evergreen shrubs with small, but spicily scented four-petalled flowers. They are special because they flower in winter and spring at a time when there is little else in flower. Unless otherwise stated they are hardy to 10°F (−12°C), US zones 8–10.

Daphne mezereum var. *rubra*

PLANTING HELP
Most daphnes come from dry woods, screes or rocky places and need good drainage, thriving in poor stony soil, especially on limestone. They are slow-growing but most are reasonably long-lived.

Daphne mezereum **var.** *rubra*
A deciduous upright bush with dusky deep pink flowers up the stems, followed by bright red fruit. A small shrub to 5ft (1.5m) high. The normal variety is purplish pink and there is a good white form. Best in well-drained, sandy soil and good on chalk. Hardy to −30°F (−35°C), US zones 4–8.

Daphne × *burkwoodii* **'Somerset Variegated'**
'Somerset' was a cross between *D. cneorum* and *D. caucasica*, raised in 1931; it is a small evergreen slow-growing shrub to 5ft (1.5m) high and wide, with most of its flowers in spring, a few later. This form has cream-edged leaves, and there is also a variety 'Gold Edge'. Hardy to −10°F (−23°C), US zones 6–9.

Daphne bholua

Daphne bholua
This is the finest of the daphnes, growing to 7ft (2m) or more, flowering in winter and early spring. The flowers are mostly formed on the ends of sparsely leaved branches, in shades of pink or white. 'Jacqueline Postill' is a very good variety. 'Gurkha' is a deciduous variety, said to be one of the hardiest. Best in acid soil in partial shade, on a north or west wall or among shrubs, and excellent in a greenhouse where the scent fills the air on a warm winter's day.

Daphne odora
A low evergreen shrub that grows to 3½ft (1m) across, famous in Chinese gardens for its scent and winter flowering. The flowers are white from red buds, in groups at the ends of the stems. A native of China, but long grown in Japan too. In **'Aureomarginata'**, which is reputed to be the hardiest clone, the leaves have a narrow, uneven pale edge. Propagate by cuttings in July.

Daphne pontica

Daphne pontica
A fast-growing (for a daphne), evergreen shrub that grows to 3½ft (1m) tall, with narrow-petalled green flowers. Easily grown, but often not long-lived, so it is wise to make new plants by layering. Good on chalk and tolerant of deep shade. Hardy to 0°F (−18°C), US zones 7–10.

Daphne odora 'Aureomarginata' flowering in March

Daphne × burkwoodii 'Somerset Variegated'

Buddleja asiatica with *Cupressus toruloas* 'Cashmeriana' in the cold conservatory at Wisley

Tender Shrubs for Early Spring

Most of the plants shown on the next four pages need the protection of a greenhouse or conservatory in cool areas, but will usually grow happily outside in areas with a Mediterranean or subtropical climate.

Buddleja

Buddleja asiatica   A shrub or small tree that grows up to 15ft (4.5m) and has thin, narrow leaves which are white on the underside. The long drooping spikes of small white flowers, scented like freesias, can be 1ft (30cm) long, and are borne from November–April. It is native to the foothills of the Himalayas and W China, where it grows on sandy river banks, scrub, roadsides and waste places. Other scented buddlejas flower in summer (*see page 82*) or autumn (*see page 92*). Hardy to 32°F (0°C), US zone 10.

PLANTING HELP   For any soil in a sheltered spot, but very frost-tender. It is good to bring into a conservatory in winter, where its freesia-like scent will fill the house. Liable to attack by red spider mite if kept indoors in summer.

Oranges & Lemons

Both of these produce delicious fruit and make extremely attractive ornamental trees, but they also have wonderfully scented, waxy white flowers in late winter and spring.

PLANTING HELP   All citrus like plenty of light and dislike sudden changes in temperature, humidity and watering patterns. If possible, provide a compost made up of equal parts of loam and leaf mould, with a little added charcoal. If the leaves start to look sooty, your plant is suffering from an infestation of scale insects; remove these by wiping the leaves with a mixture of paraffin or methylated spirits and soap or washing-up liquid.

Lemon *Citrus limon* 'Menton'   Lemons usually make small trees up to 24ft (7m) high, with glossy pale green leaves and white flowers tinged with purple on the underside. The familiar fruit is green, changing to yellow when ripe, and varies in size and exact colour according to the variety, of which there are many. Hardy to 20°F (−6°C), US zones 9–10, for short periods only.

Sweet Orange *Citrus sinensis* 'Valencia'
Sweet oranges probably originated in southern China and Vietnam and were brought to the Mediterranean area around 500 years ago. They have been cultivated for their fruit throughout the world ever since. Sweet Oranges normally grow into a small tree about 25ft (8m) high, with medium-sized glossy green leaves, rounded at the base. The deliciously fragrant flowers are waxy white and sometimes appear singly, sometimes in groups. There are numerous named varieties, including 'Valencia', which is late-fruiting. Hardy to 20°F (−6°C), US zones 9–10, for short periods only. Do not overwater in winter.

Lemon *Citrus limon* 'Menton' at Menton

Sweet Orange
Citrus sinensis 'Valencia'

Luculia

Luculia gratissima A lovely evergreen shrub from the Himalayas that grows up to 16ft (4.5m) tall. It has leathery leaves which are slightly hairy on the underside, and clusters of pink flowers, each about 1in (2.5cm) across. Hardy to 40°F (5°C), US zone 10.

PLANTING HELP Use a loam-based compost and plant in a sunny, sheltered position. Water freely during the growing season and more sparingly during winter. If the plant has been in a greenhouse, try to prune it hard and put it outside after flowering until autumn.

Luculia gratissima

Clematis armandii in Eccleston Square

Clematis

Clematis armandii This evergreen climber is native to China, where it is found scrambling through scrub, eventually reaching 25ft (8m) or more. It has beautiful glossy, dark green tapering leaves which provide a perfect foil for the clusters of starry creamy white or pinkish flowers which have a delicate scent. The variety 'Appleblossom' has the best flowers. It is reasonably hardy, to about 20°F (–6°C), US zones 9–10 or lower for short periods, but it is also a very good plant for the cool greenhouse, where the scent can be enjoyed to the full.

PLANTING HELP Does well in almost any soil, in sun or partial shade; wall protection is advisable in cooler climates. Being evergreen, this clematis is very useful for covering fences, screens, walls or unsightly structures. It requires little or no pruning, but the older woody branches need to be tied to some kind of support.

The drooping flower spikes of *Mahonia japonica*

Tobira

Pittosporum tobira
This evergreen shrub, which is native to China, Japan and Korea, usually makes a dense bush to about 10ft (3m) across but can occasionally reach 33ft (10m).

Pittosporum tobira

It has glossy, leathery, dark green leaves with a pale midrib and, from April to June, clusters of orange-blossom-scented, creamy white flowers, each about 1in (2.5cm) across. There are some variegated-leaved forms and the very compact 'Wheeler's Dwarf'. The flowers are succeeded by attractive, sticky orange seeds. Hardy to 20°F (–6°C), US zones 9–10.

PLANTING HELP *Pittosporum tobira* is widely planted in warm climates, such as the Mediterranean and California, and is popular in coastal areas as its foliage is salt-tolerant. Although not reliably hardy in N Europe, it can be grown outside successfully in mild areas in cities such as London, if given a sheltered position.

Mahonia

Mahonia japonica A well-known evergreen shrub that grows to 5ft (1.5m) tall and wide, possibly native to China but long cultivated in Japan, and in Europe since the 19th century. The rather stiff leaves have pairs of glossy, dark green leaflets with spiny margins; the long, drooping spikes of small greenish yellow flowers are wonderfully scented like Lily-of-the-valley. Hardy to 0°F (–18°C), US zones 7–10.

PLANTING HELP This shrub is easy to grow and exceptionally shade-tolerant, thus making it suitable for growing in woodland under a tree or on the north side of a wall. It prefers rich, leafy, neutral or slightly acid soil.

Acacia 'Exeter Hybrid' in the Temperate House at the Royal Botanic Gardens, Kew

Mimosa

Mimosas (or Wattles, as they are usually named in their native Australia) are part of the large genus *Acacia*, containing over 900 species of trees and shrubs native to the tropical and warm temperate areas of the world, especially Australia and Africa.

PLANTING HELP   Mimosas will normally grow in any reasonably well-drained, preferably moist, garden soil, although they will tolerate drought. They generally dislike limy soils. Though not very hardy, they can be grown outside in some northern climates with the protection of a south-facing wall. In cooler areas mimosas make some of the best winter-flowering trees for a tall conservatory or greenhouse.

Mimosa or **Silver Wattle** *Acacia dealbata*
Probably the best-known acacia, this fast-growing native of the dry forests of Australia and Tasmania makes an upright large shrub or tree to 30ft (9m). It has delicate, feathery, greyish green leaves and bears spikes of fluffy, round yellow flowers throughout the winter and spring; these are often seen for sale as cut flowers in the early part of the year. Hardy to 10°F (−12°C), US zones 8–10.

Acacia 'Exeter Hybrid'   A beautiful hybrid mimosa, this clone of *A.× veitchiana* makes a shrub or small tree up to 17ft (5m). It has slender weeping branches clothed with long, narrow, flat dark green leaves around 1in (2.5cm) long and is covered in pale yellow flowers in spikes up to 3in (8cm) long. Hardy to 32°F (0°C), US zone 10 or lower if protected from cold winds.

Mimosa
Acacia dealbata

23

Rosemary, showing the dry conditions in which it thrives

Aromatic Plants

All the plants on these two pages have aromatic foliage and their leaves need to be crushed to release their powerful scent. These low shrubs are native to dry hills in the Mediterranean region, so need full sun and well-drained soil. They will be best appreciated if they have a place near a path or seat where they can be casually crushed and sniffed.

Rosemary

Rosmarinus officinalis   A popular and well-known evergreen shrub from the Mediterranean region which grows on rocky hills and cliffs, often near the sea. It has been used for centuries as a culinary and medicinal herb, but is worth growing for its very attractive flowers and sweetly aromatic foliage. There are many forms: prostrate, low-growing and upright, with needle-like leaves and masses of small flowers in various shades of blue; all have a good scent. Hardy to 20°F (−6°C), US zones 9–10, for short periods only.

PLANTING HELP   Rosemary requires a well-drained soil and a dry, sunny position if it is to thrive. Although it can tolerate low ground temperatures for several days or even weeks, a combination of icy winds and waterlogged soil will inevitably kill it. In general, the low-growing forms are less hardy than the upright ones; those with pink and white, rather than blue flowers are also more susceptible to long periods of freezing wind. During cold weather protect plants in exposed conditions with fleece or straw.

***Rosmarinus officinalis* 'Severn Sea'**   A good variety that grows up to about 4ft (1.2m) tall and sometimes wider, with clusters of bright blue flowers in late spring. Like most rosemaries, this will eventually need plenty of space, so bear this in mind when planting. 'Benenden Blue' is similar.
'Miss Jessopp's Upright'   One of the hardiest varieties, with stiff stems to 7ft (2m) and pale blue flowers.

Cotton Lavender

Santolina is a genus of evergreen shrubs native to the Mediterranean region. Although its flowers do not appear until summer, it is valuable throughout the year for its attractive and aromatic foliage, and is often used to edge paths and borders, where the scent is released by brushing the leaves. Hardy to 0°F (−18°C), US zones 7–10.

PLANTING HELP   *Santolina* requires the same conditions as rosemary. In common with other semi-woody shrubs, it has a tendency to look scruffy with age and so will generally need replacing after a few years. A careful clip in early summer will keep it compact longer. Happily, it is quite easy to grow from cuttings taken in summer.

Santolina chamaecyparissus   A low-growing evergreen shrub that grows to about 2ft (60cm) tall and usually wider, with narrow, silvery grey leaves, covered with white felty hairs. Small, bright yellow, button-like flowers about ½in (1.5cm) across, which do nothing to enhance the beauty of the plant, are carried at the tip of slender stalks in summer.

S. pinnata subsp. *neapolitana* 'Edward Bowles'

T. × citriodorus 'Fragrantissimus'   Caraway Thyme   *R. officinalis* 'Severn Sea'

Santolina pinnata subsp. **neapolitana 'Edward Bowles'**   Similar to *Santolina chamaecyparissus*, *S. pinnata* usually makes a slightly larger plant. It also differs in its longer leaves and possibly superior scent. There are several other named forms.

Thyme

Thymes are small shrubby perennials native to Europe and the Mediterranean region. There are numerous species and named varieties, and most make rounded small shrubs of woody stems clothed with tiny aromatic leaves and clusters of pink flowers. Nearly all thymes have some scent, but we illustrate two of the best, although Common Garden Thyme *Thymus vulgaris* (*not illustrated here*) also has an excellent scent and is freely available. The shrubby species shown here are hardy to 20°F (−6°C), US zones 9–10.

Rosmarinus officinalis 'Miss Jessopp's Upright'

PLANTING HELP   Thymes need well-drained, chalky soil and a position in full sun. They should be clipped gently after flowering to keep the plants more compact.

Thymus × citriodorus 'Fragrantissimus'
This form of Lemon thyme makes a loose bush up to about 1ft (30cm) tall and 8in (20cm) wide.

Caraway Thyme *Thymus herba-barona*
A native of Corsica and Sardinia, this mat-forming plant grows up to about 1in (2.5cm) tall and 8in (20cm) wide. It puts out arching shoots that root on contact with the soil, which means that it can colonize quite a large area if left to its own devices. It has pink or mauve flowers in summer.

Santolina chamaecyparissus

E. 'Quicksilver' at the Old Vicarage, Edington

Actinidia

Actinidia kolomikta A relation of the well-known Kiwi fruit, *A. kolomikta* is a vigorous climber, native to China, Korea and Japan, where it scrambles up trees in coniferous forests. In favourable conditions it can grow up to 30ft (9m) tall. It is grown for its unusual leaves, which are heart-shaped, to 6in (15cm) long, pale green with pink and cream splashed tips. The tiny white fragrant flowers appear in late spring, smelling rather like Lily-of-the-valley; they are sometimes followed by egg-shaped yellow fruits. Hardy to −20°F (−29°C), US zones 5–9.

PLANTING HELP *Actinidia kolomikta* does best when given some support; a pergola or an arch is ideal. It will thrive in partial shade in deep, but well-drained soil.

Elaeagnus

Elaeagnus* 'Quicksilver'** An excellent large deciduous shrub or small tree that grows to 10ft (3m) tall, with oval leaves around 3in (8cm) long, silvery beneath, pale green above. Flowers with a rich, honey-like scent, silvery outside, yellow inside, appear in late spring. A larger and similar one to look out for is the Oleaster ***Elaeagnus angustifolia from the dry parts of Asia. The leaves are willow-like, silver only on the underside,

Winter's bark at Tapeley Park, Devon

Mexican orange blossom *Choisya ternata*

Elaeagnus angustifolia

Actinidia kolomikta on a shady wall in the Royal Botanic Gardens, Kew

but the flowers are, if anything, more intoxicatingly fragrant. This will eventually make a tree up to about 40ft (12m) high, so is not for the small garden. Very hardy to −40°F (−40°C), US zones 3–8.

PLANTING HELP   Both are best in very well-drained, poor soil, in a hot, dry position.

Winter's Bark

Drimys winteri   This beautiful evergreen shrub or tree has a conical habit and can eventually grow to about 50ft (16m), although it is often considerably smaller in cultivation. It grows wild in damp woods in the southern part of South America and has been known in Europe since the 16th century because its greyish, aromatic bark was formerly used by ships' doctors to prevent scurvy on long voyages round the Horn. It is rather similar in appearance to a small-leaved magnolia, and like it, has oblong, green aromatic leaves, silvery on the underside, to about 7in (18cm) long, which are clustered at the end of branches. The jasmine-scented, creamy white flowers, around 1in (2.5cm) across, appear during spring and early summer. Hardy to about 20°F (−6°C), US zones 9–10 or less, for short periods.

PLANTING HELP   *Drimys winteri* prefers a deep, moist soil and, in northern climates, a sheltered position.

Mexican Orange Blossom

Choisya ternata   An evergreen shrub native to Mexico that grows up to 10ft (3m) tall. The glossy green leaflets are grouped in threes and if crushed, give off a strong, not particularly pleasant, smell. The flowers, however, which are white and held in clusters, are deliciously, if delicately scented. These appear mainly during the spring, although a second batch is often produced in autumn. *Choisya ternata* is surprisingly hardy and will usually survive temperatures down to 0°F (−18°C), US zones 7–10 or lower for short periods.

PLANTING HELP   Try to provide a sheltered site and well-drained soil. It is rather fast-growing and will reshoot well when pruned quite hard.

Viburnums

This large genus of shrubs is hard to beat for its ease of cultivation and attractive, often scented, flowers. There are at least 100 different species and many more named hybrids and varieties, and as they are mostly found in mountainous areas, they tend to grow well in cool climates. Deciduous viburnums are generally very hardy down to −10°F (−23°C), US zones 6–9. We illustrate some of the best-scented ones here (*see also page 9*), but there are many others worth a place in the garden, among them the evergreens *Viburnum japonicum* and *Viburnum odoratissimum*.

PLANTING HELP   Most viburnums do best in full sun in a good, deep, rich, moist soil, but we have a fine healthy specimen of *V.× burkwoodii* growing in our N Devon garden on appalling stony soil in full sun.

***Viburnum × burkwoodii* 'Park Farm Hybrid'**
One of the early hybrid viburnums, this grows to about 8ft (2.5m) tall and wide. It is hardier and faster growing than its parent *V. carlesii* and has semi-evergreen, rough, ovate green leaves which are brown on the underside. The small flowers, pinkish becoming white, appear in early spring and are carried in rounded clusters about 3in (8cm) across.

***Viburnum* 'Anne Russell'**   This variety is what is known as a backcross of *V. carlesii* and *V.× burkwoodii*, which explains why it is sometimes listed in books and catalogues under *V. carlesii* and sometimes under *V.× burkwoodii*. It is a good, compact, very fragrant shrub that grows to about 6ft (1.8m) eventually, with flower clusters to about 3in (8cm) wide, white from pink buds.

Viburnum carlesii
One of the most beautiful and fragrant viburnums, this deciduous species is native to Japan and Korea. It makes a rounded bush to about 5ft (1.5m) tall and wide. The leaves are broadly ovate, and the very fragrant flowers, which are pinkish at first, then white, are carried in clusters to about 3in (8cm) wide in early spring.

'Anne Russell'

Viburnum × juddii   This hybrid between *V. carlesii* and *V. bitchiuense*, makes a rounded shrub to about 7ft (2m) tall. In spring it has larger and looser heads of smaller flowers than *V. carlesii* and not quite such a powerful scent.

Viburnum carlesii

Viburnum × burkwoodii
'Park Farm Hybrid'

Viburnum × juddii

Viburnum carlesii by the river in the garden at Ninfa, southeast of Rome

Viburnum × juddii on poor stony soil in Devon

Lily-of-the-valley *Convallaria majalis*

Sweet Woodruff *Galium odoratum*

Lily-of-the-valley

Lily-of-the-valley *Convallaria majalis*
This must be one of the best-known and most-loved of all scented plants, and *parfumiers* through the ages have tried to capture the essence of its uniquely sweet smell. It is best seen growing in drifts in woodland or dappled shade in the garden, but we have also grown it successfully in a pot indoors; prepared rhizomes can be bought especially for this purpose. Lily-of-the-valley is native to Europe and North America, where it grows in woods and scrub on limestone and sandy soils. It has slender stems to 8in (20cm) with soft green leaves and 5–13 tiny bell-shaped white flowers. Several varieties are found in the wild and others have been raised or selected over the years. **'Fortin's Giant'** is a large clone, while a pink-flowered variety, *C. majalis* var. *rosea* is also available. Hardy to −10°F (−23°C), US zones 6–9.

PLANTING HELP   Lily-of-the-valley can be difficult to establish, but we have found that it does best planted outside in partial shade, in good rich, moist soil, with added leaf mould, if possible. Make a shallow depression in the soil, gently place the rhizomes in it, carefully spreading out the roots, and pile loose leaf mould on top to completely cover the plant. If left undisturbed, the plants will form spreading mats.

Lily-of-the-valley

Sarcococca hookeriana

Sarcococca confusa

Sweet Woodruff

Galium odoratum   Sweet Woodruff has a pleasant hay-like scent which becomes more pronounced with drying and has been used for many centuries as a strewing herb, moth repellent and ingredient of pot pourri. It is native to woods in Europe and North Africa and is a mat-forming perennial, with numerous slender stems to about 8in (20cm) tall. The bright green leaves are arranged in whorls and the tiny white tubular, 4-petalled flowers, which are also scented, appear in clusters in early summer. Hardy to 0°F (−18°C), US zones 7–9.

PLANTING HELP   Sweet Woodruff does well in cool, shady situations, and is very invasive, spreading by means of creeping underground stolons, so it makes good ground-cover for tricky areas under trees and hedges.

Sarcococca

This genus of evergreen shrubs, sometimes called Sweet Box or Christmas Box, is native to the Himalayas and China. There are several species and varieties available, most of which have small, but very fragrant flowers in early spring often followed by black berries.

PLANTING HELP   Sarcococcas do best in good, moist soil in partial shade, but will also tolerate drier, sunnier conditions. They are valuable for shady places near the house or can be grown in a pot and brought indoors when in flower to scent a room.

Sarcococca confusa   A branching evergreen shrub that grows to 7ft (2m) tall and wide. The leathery leaves are dark green on the upper side, lighter green below. Sweetly scented flowers appear in early spring and are followed by attractive red berries which turn black when ripe. Hardy to 10°F (−12°C), US zones 8–10.

Sarcococca hookeriana   This tough plant from the forests of the eastern Himalayas is easily grown on acid soils, making a thicket of stems up to 3½ft (1m) tall. It has bright green, narrow leaves and small, scented flowers in early spring. A very similar plant, *S. hookeriana* var. *digyna* (*not illustrated*) is also available; it has a good scent, is hardier and more compact than var. *hookeriana*. Hardy to 0°F (−18°C), US zones 7–10.

Flowering Currants

Currants and gooseberries are well known in the fruit garden, but some species are also popular as ornamental garden plants. Most, such as *Ribes sanguineum*, have leaves with a distinctive smell, others have scented flowers.

Flowering Currant

PLANTING HELP   Currants are easy to grow in reasonably good, moist, but well-drained soil in full sun or semi-shade. Cut back after flowering to maintain a decent-shaped bush.

Buffalo Currant *Ribes odoratum*   A spreading deciduous shrub that grows to about 7ft (2m) tall and is native to the midwest of North America, where it grows along streams. It is spineless with pale green, 3-lobed leaves and hanging clusters of spicily scented, bright yellowish green flowers in April. This is the best *Ribes* for flower scent and is a very attractive plant, endearing itself to the gardener by its habit of flowering while still young. The variety 'Crandall' also has edible fruit. Very hardy down to −20°F (−29°C), US zones 5–9.

Ribes × gordonianum   This is the hybrid between *Ribes odoratum* and *Ribes sanguineum*. It forms a large, much-branched shrub to 8ft (2.5m) tall, covered with orange to pinkish flowers in spring. Though both parents are American, this hybrid was first raised in England in 1837. Hardy to −20°F (−29°C), US zones 5–9.

Flowering Currant *Ribes sanguineum*
This deciduous shrub is native to western North America where it grows in open woodland, 3½–10ft (1–3m) tall, with rounded, dark green leaves and hanging clusters of white, pink or red flowers. It is useful for producing scores of flowers early in the year at a time when most gardens lack colour. Although the flowers themselves lack scent, the whole bush gives off a wonderful aroma of blackcurrants, which is especially pronounced in warm, sunny conditions. There are several named varieties available (*not illustrated*), including 'Tydeman's White' (pale flowers), 'Brocklebankii' (golden leaves and pale flowers), and 'King Edward VII' (similar to 'Pulborough Scarlet', but makes a smaller bush and flowers a little later). Hardy to about 0°F(−18°C), US zones 7–10.
'Pulborough Scarlet' is a tall, brightly coloured variety that grows up to 10ft (3m).

Lonicera

Although most people think of climbing plants when they hear the word honeysuckle, there are

Ribes sanguineum
'Pulborough Scarlet'

Ribes × gordonianum in Sellindge, Kent

SHRUBBY HONEYSUCKLES

Buffalo Currant *Ribes odoratum* in the authors' garden in Kent

Flowering Currant *Ribes sanguineum*

also a number of shrubby species which are worth growing for their scent in spring. These early-flowering, shrubby species are hardy to −20°F (−29°C), US zones 5–9.

PLANTING HELP   Honeysuckles will grow in ordinary garden soil, in sun or partial shade, but will produce more flowers in sun.

Lonicera × purpusii   This hybrid between two other shrubby honeysuckles makes a rounded, deciduous shrub that grows to 10ft (3m) tall. The fragrant, creamy white flowers, around ½in (1.5cm) long, are carried in small clusters up the stems very early in the year (usually from February onwards). Definitely grown for its scent rather than looks.

Lonicera × purpusii

Pelargonium 'Sweet Mimosa' is one of the hardiest and most free-flowering of the scented pelargoniums

Scented Pelargoniums

There are around 250 species of *Pelargonium*, part of the *Geranium* family. Most pelargoniums come from South Africa and are perennials or small, often succulent shrubs, though a few are annuals. Pelargoniums are very popular all over the world for their attractive flowers, grown outside in warm areas or as greenhouse plants in temperate climates. There are numerous varieties with interestingly scented leaves and a few with scented flowers. Most pelargoniums flower in late spring and early summer and many will continue into autumn provided the dead flowers are removed regularly. Some, such as 'Sweet Mimosa', are seldom without a flower.

PLANTING HELP   Most pelargoniums do best in well-drained gritty, sandy soils in full sun; they dislike cold, wet conditions and stagnant air. Avoid waterlogging and keep them almost dry in dull, cold weather. They prove rather tender in most temperate zones, so will need protection from frost. When planted in large pots, they can stand outside in summer in the sunny, airy conditions which they like, before being moved under cover for the winter.

'Citriodorum' (syn. 'Queen of Lemons') An attractive, softly hairy, free-flowering variety that grows to 3½ft (1m) or more with support. The leaves are shallowly 3-lobed with toothed edges; the flowers are silvery mauve with darker markings on the two upper petals, produced in late spring and early summer. Hardy to 32°F (0°C), US zone 10.

'Mabel Grey'   A form of the South African *Pelargonium citronellum*, as the name suggests, has sharply lemon-scented leaves. It has rough, pale

Pelargonium 'Citriodorum' with 'Village Hill Oak'

Pelargonium tomentosum naturalized on Tresco

Rose Geranium *Pelargonium* 'Graveolens'

green, deeply cut leaves and heads of small, pale pink flowers, with deeper pink markings in spring. Although easy to grow, this variety is often susceptible to botrytis in damp, stagnant air, especially in winter, so it needs to be grown in light, sunny, airy place. It is hardy to 32°F (0°C), US zone 10.

Pelargonium tomentosum A native to the SW Cape area of South Africa, this robust, spreading and clambering plant grows to 7ft (2m) or more. It has very soft, hairy, pale green, peppermint-scented leaves and clusters of very small, pale pink or white flowers. Needs ample water, but otherwise easy to grow. Hardy to about 32°F (0°C), US zone 10.

Rose Geranium *Pelargonium* 'Graveolens' This old rose-scented cultivar is commonly grown for its essential oil, known as Oil of Geranium, which is used in perfumery and aromatherapy as a substitute for the very expensive Attar of Roses. It has deeply divided, mid-green leaves and heads of pale pink flowers with darker markings. Easy to grow. Hardy to about 24°F (−5°C), US zone 10.

'Sweet Mimosa' This robust and free-flowering variety, raised from a cross between the Oak-leaf Geranium (*see next entry*) and a large-flowered variety, is sometimes grouped with the

pelargoniums known as Uniques. The divided leaves are wonderfully aromatic, while the pale rose pink flowers are produced non-stop throughout the year. Hardy down to about 24°F (−5°C), US zone 10 and the warmer parts of zone 9.

'Village Hill Oak' This is one of several cultivated forms of the scented Oak-leaf Geranium, *Pelargonium quercifolium*, a species from South Africa. 'Village Hill Oak' has softly hairy, deeply lobed leaves, around 2½in (6cm) across, slightly sticky and smelling of balsam. The pale pink flowers with dark purple markings, are carried in tight clusters from spring to autumn. Hardy to around 24°F (−5°C), US zones 10 and the warmer parts of zone 9.

'Mabel Grey'

Perennial Honesty *Lunaria rediviva*

White Perennial Stock *Matthiola incana*

Sweet Rocket *Hesperis matronalis*

Mixed biennial wallflowers

Dame's Violet

Sweet Rocket *Hesperis matronalis*   This biennial or short-lived perennial has white, pink or lilac flowers on tall stems, to about 4ft (1.2m) in May and June. The scent is best in the evening. Dame's Violet has been a popular cottage garden plant for many centuries and has become wild in many areas, especially those with cool summers, such as Scotland, where it can make a fine show along banks and ditches. Hardy to about −10°F (−23°C), US zones 6–9.

PLANTING HELP   Like the white stock, this plant usually lasts for a few years before becoming exhausted. Once this happens and flowering starts to diminish, it is best to raise new plants from seed, which is straightforward with the single-flowered type. The double-flowered form, which must be propagated by cuttings, is unfortunately more difficult to grow. Does well on moist, peaty soil, unlike the stocks and wallflowers.

Wallflowers

Wallflowers are one of the typical old-fashioned flowers of spring, long used in cottage gardens or in bedding schemes with bulbs, especially tulips, and forget-me-nots, all three flowering together. All wallflowers are scented, but the ordinary varieties, and especially the yellows, have better scent than the perennial varieties such as 'Bowles' Mauve'. Probably hardy to about 0°F (−18°C), US zones 7–10.

PLANTING HELP   Sow seed in early spring and in autumn transplant to the place in which they are to flower. Propagate these perennials by cuttings. This plant is found growing wild on Roman and medieval walls throughout much of Europe. It thrives in dry, well-drained, preferably limy, soils and will not tolerate waterlogged conditions.

Wallflower *Erysimum cheiri* (syn. *Cheiranthus cheiri*)   This perennial, often grown as a biennial, is native to the eastern Mediterranean region, where it grows on cliffs and rocks. It normally makes a compact, rather shrub-like plant up to about 1ft (30cm) tall, but garden varieties can attain nearly double that height. The velvety flowers are yellow in the wild, but in cultivated forms vary from pink and cream, through yellow and orange, to red and brown; single colours or even a mixed display can look very attractive.

Stocks

White Perennial Stock *Matthiola incana*
This form of the wild stock is one of the most easily grown and powerfully scented of all garden flowers. The scent is best in the evening. The stout stem grows up to about 1ft (30cm) tall, topped by soft greyish leaves, and carries numerous flowering stems and a succession of flowers. If the faded flowers are cut off, more are produced into autumn. Each plant lasts 3–5 years, finally reaching 3½ft (1m) tall. The white form is the commonest, but there is also a deep purple-flowered strain. Probably hardy to about 0°F (−18°C), US zones 7–10.

PLANTING HELP   Well-drained, sandy or chalky soil suits this plant best.

Perennial Honesty

Perennial Honesty *Lunaria rediviva*   Unlike the other plants on this page, this Honesty is a long-lived, clump-forming perennial. The flowering stems, which grow up to about 3½ft (1m), emerge in spring, elongating during flowering with white or very pale pink flowers and a few later flowers throughout the summer. The lovely scent floats on the evening air. The seed pods are papery, like the familiar biennial Honesty, but are smaller and narrowly elliptical. Hardy to about −10°F (−23°C), US zones 6–9.

PLANTING HELP   This needs deep, rich, moist soil, with shade in the middle of the day.

Wallflowers planted with white tulips at Hever Castle in Kent

Pontic Azalea on the Georgian Military Highway

Rhododenrons & Azaleas

Three different groups of rhododendrons are renowned for their scent: the deciduous azaleas, the tender, scented rhododendrons with large white flowers often called Maddeniis; and the tree-like evergreen rhododendrons with pale flowers, of which the most familiar is *Rhododendron × loderi*. The Maddeniis are especially useful in areas such as California and Australia, as they are more heat- and drought-tolerant than the other groups; they also make excellent pot plants in a cool conservatory.

PLANTING HELP   All rhododendrons and azaleas do best in acid, sandy soil, and if grown in pots, need watering with rainwater. Special peat composts mixed with sand and ground bark, make an ideal potting mix. If you are growing these plants in pots, they should be stood outside in a shady place in summer.

Azalea **'George Reynolds'**   A robust deciduous shrub that grows to 10ft (3m) with large heads of scented flowers to 9in (23cm) across. Easily grown in sandy soil. Hardy to about −10°F (−23°C), US zones 6–9.

Pontic Azalea *Rhododendron luteum*   This species is one of the best for scent, with relatively small flowers in a head to 5in (12cm) across. It can grow to 10ft (3m), though it is usually around 5ft (1.5m). It will grow well on neutral soil, provided it has plenty of humus. Hardy to about −20°F (−29°C), US zones 5–9.

Rhododendron **'Countess of Haddington'**
This old variety makes an evergreen shrub up to 6ft (1.8m) tall. It has dark green leaves, scaly on

Rhododendron 'Countess of Haddington'

Rhododendron fortunei subsp. *discolor*

A fine planting of *Azalea* 'George Reynolds' in Eccleston Square, with the cherry 'Kanzan', behind

the underside, and bears large, funnel-shaped white flowers flushed with pink during April–May. A good one for a tub in the conservatory or a warm garden outside. Hardy to 20°F (–6°C), US zones 9–10.

Rhododendron fortunei subsp. *discolor*
This is one of a group of large rhododendrons that grows to 30ft (10m) with smooth, evergreen leaves and large white flowers in loose clusters around 5in (12cm) across. Native to much of central China, so hardy, tolerant of neutral soil and heat, and often rather late-flowering. The scent is sharp with overtones of medicinal witchhazel. Hardy to 0°F (–18°C), US zones 7–10.

Rhododendron × loderi 'Venus'
The × *loderi* group of hybrid Rhododendrons combine the good features of the parents, *R. fortunei* and *R. griffithianum*. The flowers are freely produced, large and with the medicinal witchhazel scent. In 'Venus' each flower is pink in bud, opening pale pink, around 5in (12cm across). It forms a large, rounded evergreen shrub to 20ft (6m) across. Best in moist, acid soil, with dappled shade in warm areas. Hardy to 0°F (–18°C), US zones 7–10.

Rhododendron × loderi 'Venus'

Iris 'Jane Phillips' with *Stachys byzantina*

Iris pallida in an old kitchen garden

Iris 'Amethyst Flame'

Iris 'Joyce Terny'

Bearded Irises

Bearded irises have been much developed by breeders in the past hundred years and now have large flowers in a greater range of colours than could have been imagined when breeding began. The most modern have lost something of the elegance of the old varieties, but many have gained the ability to flower in autumn as well as in early summer – the so-called 'remontants'. All share a violet-like scent to the flower. The old white-flowered *Iris* 'Florentina', an albino form of the deep blue *Iris germanica*, is the source of orris root which is extracted from the dried rhizomes and is much used in perfumery and pot pourri. All are hardy to 0°F (−18°C), US zones 7–10.

PLANTING HELP   Bearded irises originate on rocky limestone hills around the Mediterranean and need well-drained but rich soil with ample chalk or limestone rubble or gravel. They must be divided every 4–5 years, in summer after the plants have flowered. If slugs are common in the garden, put sand around the rhizomes to protect the young roots which emerge in late summer.

Iris pallida   An easily-grown iris with tall stems to 3½ft (1m). The pale blue flowers, around 4in (10cm) across, emerge from papery white bracts,

Bearded irises in Eccleston Square

in succession for about a month. The fan of wide bluish green leaves to 18in (45cm) tall, is also attractive. Native to the Adriatic coast of Bosnia.

Iris **'Amethyst Flame'** A modern variety with stems to 3½ft (1m). Flowers ruffled, deep lavender blue with brown markings on the lower petals.

Iris **'Ballyhoo'** A modern variety raised in 1970 with stems to 2½ft (75cm). Flowers ruffled, pale ochre yellow with the lower petals pinky purple, marked with maroon and ochre.

Iris 'Ballyhoo' at David Austin's nursery

Iris **'Champagne Elegance'** A new variety raised in 1986 with stems to 3½ft (1m). Flowers ruffled, peachy pink with the upper petals white.

Iris **'Jane Phillips'** A relatively old variety raised in 1946 with stems to 3½ft (1m). Lovely, large, pure sky blue flowers with a pale yellow beard.

Iris **'Joyce Terny'** A modern variety raised in 1974 with stems to 3½ft (1m). Flowers large, ruffled, yellow with a white centre to all the petals and a deep yellow beard.

Iris 'Champagne Elegance'

Brooms

Spanish Broom
Spartium junceum
A native of Portugal and
the Mediterranean region,
where it is usually found on
scrubby hillsides, it grows very
rapidly to 10ft (3m) or more. It
has stiff, rush-like stems, sparsely
clad with a few narrow, rather
insignificant leaves. The flowering
season is very long, from late May
or early June until September, and
the fragrant yellow pea-like
flowers are in clusters up to 18in
(45cm) long. Hardy to 0°F
(−18°C), US zones 7–10.

Spanish
Broom

PLANTING HELP
Spanish Broom will grow in
most soils, but does best in a well-drained position
in full sun; it is also valuable for seaside gardens.
To obtain a good crop of flowers cut back hard in
the autumn once it has finished flowering.
Incidentally, it dislikes being moved once
established in the garden, so try to put it in the
right place first time around.

Genista cinerea Although not the commonest
broom, this is one of the most desirable and is
worth searching for. It is a deciduous shrub that
grows to about 12ft (3.5m), native to SW Europe
and North Africa, where it inhabits dry, high-
altitude hillsides. The twiggy branches are thinly

clothed with narrow, greyish green leaves, while
the small clusters of attractive little yellow flowers
appear in May and June and are particularly well-
scented. Hardy to 0°F (−18°C), US zones 7–10.

PLANTING HELP   Good for a hot, dry place.

Cytisus battandieri This distinctive deciduous
shrub is something of an odd man out among
the brooms. It is native to Morocco, where it
grows in sandy, acid soil and makes a large, semi-
evergreen bush, up to about 13ft (4m), with rather
spindly branches and large silvery, downy leaves.
The dense spikes of golden yellow flowers, to
about 4in (10cm) long, have a strong scent, often
likened to that of pineapple.

PLANTING HELP   Good in poor, well-
drained soil in full sun; in cool, windy climates it is
often best grown against a warm wall. Cut back
old feeble stems after flowering. Like the other
brooms, this does not transplant well, and is best
bought as a container plant and put straight into
its final position in the garden. Hardy to 0°F
(−18°C), US zones 7–10.

Wisteria

Wisterias are beautiful climbing deciduous shrubs
with long, hanging clusters of bluish pea-like
flowers, often seen scrambling over walls and
buildings. There are several species and many
different forms and hybrids available, nearly all of
which have deliciously spice-scented flowers.
Hardy to −10°F (−23°C), US zones 6–9.

Cytisus battandieri

Wisteria floribunda 'Alba'

Genista cinerea

Wisteria sinensis

Wisteria sinensis in Monet's garden at Giverny

PLANTING HELP Wisterias are usually best trained against a wall or over an arch, pergola or outhouse. If unchecked, they can grow to be extremely large, with stout stems climbing into trees, so it is important to provide a really strong support. Wisterias like good, moist soil, although a poorer soil will keep growth under control; in either case, they do not do well on really chalky soils. Late frosts may kill the flower buds.

Wisteria floribunda This species is native to Japan where it grows in woods and along streams, flowering from about May to July. It can grow up to 30ft (9m) or more high, and is notable for its extremely long racemes of scented pale mauve flowers, up to 2ft (60cm) long, but as much as a dramatic 5ft (1.5m) in some of the cultivated forms, collectively known as 'Macrobotrys' (or, more recently 'Multijuga'). There are a number of other forms with flowers of different colours, including a pretty white one, 'Alba', and 'Rosea', with pink flowers. Hardy to −10°F (−23°C), US zones 6–9.

Wisteria sinensis The Chinese wisteria flowers earlier and often for a shorter period than *Wisteria floribunda*, usually in April–May, and sometimes produces a second, poorer crop of flowers a couple of months later. It can eventually climb up to 120ft (40m), and also differs from the Japanese wisteria by twining around objects in an anticlockwise direction. Again, there are a number of forms and hybrids with different coloured flowers. Hardy to 0°F (−18°C), US zones 7–10.

'Sensation'

'Katherine
Havemeyer'

'Mme Antoine
Buchner'

'Maud
Notcutt'

Specimens from Eccleston Square

Lilacs

Lilacs are a traditional feature of gardens in late spring, well-known for their evocative scent and beautiful flowers. There are about 25 species of *Syringa*, but the best known is the Common Lilac, which was a particular favourite of the Victorians; trees planted over a hundred years ago can still be seen in the gardens of large country houses and of consulates along the Silk Road. In addition to those described below, some others (*not illustrated here*) have a good scent, but are less commonly available. These include the Rouen Lilac *Syringa × chinensis*, which flowers earlier than the Common Lilac; *S. × hyacinthiflora* 'Esther Staley', a free-flowering hybrid with single pink flowers; and the free-flowering *S. microphylla* 'Superba', with very small leaves and heads of sweetly scented lilac flowers. Most are very hardy to −30°F (−35°C), US zones 4–8.

Syringa vulgaris 'Sensation'

Syringa × persica 'Alba'

Syringa vulgaris 'Katherine Havemeyer' in Eccleston Square

PLANTING HELP Lilacs prefer a sunny position in good, well-drained soil; they do particularly well on chalk and dislike very acid conditions. They usually take 2–3 years to become established after planting, so do not expect wonderful flowers immediately. If you have the time, it is a good idea to cut off the dead blooms, which will help to boost the production of flowers in the following season and maintain the shape of the bush.

Persian Lilac *Syringa × persica* An ancient hybrid cultivated since early times in India and Iran (Persia). This makes a dense, rounded bush that grows to about 6ft (1.8m) tall with small, scented, pale lilac flowers in May. The white form 'Alba' (*shown here*) was raised in the 18th century and has proved to be a hardy and attractive shrub with good scent.

Common Lilac *Syringa vulgaris* A deciduous shrub that grows to 12ft (3.5m) or more, this has been grown in W Europe for at least two centuries, but is native to E Europe where it grows on rocky hills. The green heart-shaped leaves are up to 6in (15cm) long, while the white or pale mauve flowers are carried in clusters up to 8in (20cm) long. Those illustrated here are a few of the hundreds of varieties of the Common Lilac and are both good and easy to obtain.

'Katherine Havemeyer' A very popular compact variety with dense heads of large, double, pale lavender purple flowers, which fade on opening.

'Mme Antoine Buchner' A tall shrub with a rather open habit and double, pale rose purple flowers in long trusses.

'Maud Notcutt' An upright shrub with flat, single white flowers in large flower heads up to 1ft (30cm) long.

'Sensation' A flashy lilac with a rather lax habit and reddish purple flowers edged with white.

Philadelphus coronarius, one of the strongest-scented and earliest-flowering species

Philadelphus 'Avalanche'

Philadelphus

Philadelphus or Mock Orange is a genus of deciduous shrubs, valuable in the garden for their long-lasting, sweetly scented flowers and their graceful habit of growth. All have white flowers, with or without pinkish markings in the throat, and are carried, sometimes singly, sometimes in clusters, at the ends of short branches, during June and July. In general, the garden hybrids have as good a scent as the species.

Philadelphus 'Belle Etoile'

Philadelphus 'Sybille'

PLANTING HELP *Philadelphus* grows well in good fertile soil, in sun or partial shade. It is important to realise that next year's flowers are borne on the long soft young shoots which are formed after flowering, so try to avoid cutting these back, concentrating instead on getting rid of woody old branches that have flowered already.

PHILADELPHUS

Philadelphus coronarius A dense bush that grows to 10ft (3m) tall. It is native to SE Europe where it grows on rocky hillsides and has been grown in Britain since the 16th century. The creamy white, heavily scented flowers appear in May and June, earlier than some others. Hardy to −20°F (−29°C), US zones 5–9.

Philadelphus microphyllus A compact rounded bush that grows to 4ft (1.2m) tall and is native to the SW of the USA, where it grows in dry, sunny, rocky places. A distinct species with very small leaves, it bears pure white pineapple-scented flowers in June and July. It tends to flower better in warmer areas. Hardy to −10°F (−23°C), US zones 6–9.

Garden Hybrids There are numerous hybrids between the species, some of which occurred naturally and many of which were raised by plantsmen such as the great French plant breeder Victor Lemoine (1823–1912). All the hybrids shown here are hardy to about 0°F (−18°C), US zones 7–10.

'Avalanche' An arching, spreading shrub that grows to 7ft (2m) with small flowers to about 1in (2.5cm) across, borne in clusters.

'Beauclerk' A robust, spreading, elegant shrub that grows to 7ft (2m) or more, with arching branches and large flowers that open out flat, up to 3in (8cm) across, white with a pinkish tinge at the base.

'Belle Etoile' One of the best of the hybrids, this makes a free-flowering bush to about 5ft (1.5m) tall. The large creamy white flowers have a reddish mauve blotch in the centre.

'Sybille' This very charming hybrid is similar to 'Belle Etoile', but has more cup-shaped flowers on a smaller bush, with arching stems to 3½ft (1m).

Philadelphus 'Avalanche' in Eccleston Square

Philadelphus 'Beauclerk'

Philadelphus microphyllus

Magnolias

Magnolias have some of the largest and most fragrant flowers of all the trees hardy in temperate climates. A genus of trees and large shrubs, some deciduous and others evergreen, magnolias are native to eastern Asia and southeastern North America.

PLANTING HELP   Unlike most other trees and shrubs, magnolias are best transplanted during the late spring, as the fleshy roots, which are easily damaged, repair themselves more quickly then. They normally thrive in good, moist, but not waterlogged soil, and although most species are perfectly hardy in northern Europe, the flowers are susceptible to damage by late frosts.

Magnolia × wiesneri (syn. *Magnolia × watsoni*) A medium-sized deciduous tree, slow-growing to 20ft (6m) and eventually more, a probable hybrid between *M. hypoleuca* and *M. sieboldii*, flowering in June and July. The leaves, to 18in (45cm) long, are paler and slightly downy underneath. The large, creamy white, strongly scented flowers have a mass of a bright purplish red stamens in the centre, and are up to 8in (20cm) across. Hardy to −10°F (−23°C), US zones 6–9.

Magnolia sieboldii   Native to S Japan and Korea where it grows in woods in the mountains; a large deciduous shrub to 13ft (4m) high, with broadly ovate leaves, dark green above and downy blue green underneath, up to about 6in (15cm) long. The wonderfully scented, cup-shaped flowers, up to 4in (10cm) across, on long stalks, appear intermittently from May to July. They are pure white with numerous dark crimson stamens forming a pronounced central splash of colour. Does best in lime-free conditions. Hardy to −10°F (−23°C), US zones 6–9.

Magnolia sinensis (syn. *M. sieboldii* subsp. *sinensis*)   A deciduous tree or shrub with a spreading habit that grows to 20ft (6m) tall, *Magnolia sinensis* is native to China where it grows in scrubby forests at high altitudes. The broadly obovate leaves are bright green, up to 6in (15cm) long. The white flowers appear in June and are saucer-shaped, to about 5in (12cm) across. Tolerates chalky soils. Hardy to 0°F (−18°C), US zones 7–10.

Magnolia stellata   This deciduous species is smaller than the two mentioned earlier, usually making a bush no more than 15ft (4.5m) tall after many years. It is native to Japan where it grows in

Magnolia wilsonii at Benmore, Argyll

Magnolia stellata

Magnolia sinensis

Magnolia sieboldii

woods in the mountains, flowering in late March or April. The young bark is aromatic. *Magnolia stellata* is wonderfully free-flowering from an early age; the scented, pure white flowers with their strap-shaped petals appearing on almost every branch. The one drawback is that they are easily spoilt by frost, wind or rain. There are several different named cultivars of this species, some with pale pink flowers. Hardy to 0°F (−18°C), US zones 7–10.

Magnolia wilsonii Similar to *Magnolia sinensis*, this beautiful deciduous shrub or small tree grows to about 24ft (7m). It is native to China where it grows in scrub and moist forest at high altitudes, which accounts for its preference for shade or partial shade in the garden. The leaves are ovate, to 6in (15cm) long, green on the upper side, softly brown underneath. The pendulous cup-shaped flowers appear in May and June, and are white, to 3in (9cm) or more across, with a central boss of bright red stamens and a wonderful scent. Good on chalky soils. Hardy to 0°F (−18°C), US zones 7–10, but the flowers are very susceptible to frost.

Magnolia × wiesneri

The opening flowers of *Zaluzianskya ovata*

Evening Primrose *Oenothera biennis*

Night-scented Flowers

Strong night scents which fill the air are often produced by insignificant or white flowers. In most cases the scents are designed to attract night-flying moths. Insignificant flowers hide themselves in the day, but often open at night; and while white flowers are conspicuous to man, they are relatively inconspicuous to insects by day, and show up much better at night.

Impatiens

Impatiens tinctoria A large perennial native to east and central Africa, growing in rainforest in the mountains. This has fleshy roots and several tall stems to 6ft (1.8m), topped by large, long-spurred white flowers, around 2in (5cm) across, with red streaks in the throat; scented in the evening. Hardy to 20°F (–6 °C), US zones 9–10.

PLANTING HELP   Best in a partially shaded place in good, rich soil. The tuberous roots should be protected from frost with a layer of peat or straw, or brought indoors in winter. The shoot tips are often damaged by capsid bug.

Night-scented Stocks

Matthiola longipetala* subsp. *bicornis
Although the curled purplish flowers of Night-scented Stocks are insignificant in the daytime, in the evening their scent fills the air. They are annuals, found wild in sandy and rocky places from the eastern Mediterranean to Arabia. In gardens they grow to around 1ft (30cm) tall with the open flowers to 2in (5cm) across. Plant them under a window or near where people will walk on warm summer nights. A few stems, picked and brought indoors, will scent a room. Hardy to 20°F (–6°C), US zones 9–10.

PLANTING HELP   Sow seeds in autumn or spring in rich sandy soil where they are to flower. Keep moist until flowering when the plants should be drier.

Night-scented Stocks

Impatiens tinctoria in Cornwall

Night-scented cactus *Epiphyllum crenatum*

Evening Primrose

Oenothera biennis   A variable species with stems that grow to 6ft (1.8m) or more, and a succession of large, pale yellow flowers, which open around sundown and are usually fading by morning. The evening scent is sweet but delicate. Hardy to –30°F (–35°C), US zones 4–10.

PLANTING HELP   Easily grown from seed in any soil in full sun. The plants are biennial, forming a stemless rosette of leaves the first year, and a leafy flowering stem the second.

Night-scented Cactus

Epiphyllum crenatum   An epiphytic cactus with clumps of upright or arching stems that grows to around 20in (50cm). The large white flowers, 8in (20cm) long, 4in (10cm) across the inner petals, are so fragrant in the evening that they scent the whole room. A native to Mexico and Honduras, growing on rocks and trees, flowering in spring. The Kang Hua *Epiphyllum oxypetalum* is a taller plant with arching stems to 6ft (1.8m) and large white flowers, fragrant in the evening. It is commonly cultivated in SE Asia. Both are hardy to 32°F (0°C), US zone 10.

PLANTING HELP   Easily grown in sandy, leafy soil in a pot or hanging basket, watered in summer, dry in winter.

Pelargonium

Pelargonium gibbosum   A strange plant with stick-like stems that grow to 3½ft (1m) or more, scrambling through bushes by the sea along the west coast of South Africa. The bluish green leaves are attractive; the small green flowers in a loose umbel, are strongly scented in the evening, like cheap soap. *Pelargonium triste*, a tuberous plant with feathery leaves and brownish flowers in spring and summer, also has a good scent in the evening. Both are hardy to 32°F (0°C), US zone 10.

PLANTING HELP   Sow seeds in autumn. *Pelargonium gibbosum* is also easy to propagate from stem cuttings; *P. triste* from bits of fleshy root. For dry sandy soil, watered in winter, dry in summer.

Zaluzianskya

Zaluzianskya ovata   A rather tender perennial that forms a a mound to 1ft (30cm) across, of sticky, acrid-smelling leaves, but topped by white heavily scented flowers to 1in (2.5cm) across, that open in the evening or on dark days from knob-shaped red buds. Native to stony places in the Drakensberg Mountains in South Africa.

PLANTING HELP   Good in a pot in the greenhouse, to be taken indoors in flower. Can be grown outside in a windy pocket to keep moulds at bay. Hardy to 20°F (–6°C), US zones 9–10.

Pelargonium gibbosum

Dianthus

This is an enormous genus with more than 300 species and over 30,000 cultivars. For ease of reference, the cultivars are normally divided into two groups, carnations and pinks, which in turn are subdivided into groups including Annual, Border, Perpetual-flowering, Spray and Malmaison carnations, and Annual, Biennial and Alpine pinks. There are also a number of plants which do not really fall happily into any of these groups, and there is always a great deal of debate about which, if any, of the above are truly perennial, and therefore long-lasting in the garden. Some idea of the different groups will help you buy the type of plant you actually want. Incidentally, any pink or carnation with 'clove' or 'spice' in its name, will have a good scent.

Garden Pinks

Garden pinks are attractive, usually old varieties, which make low clumps of greyish foliage. Most, like the well-known **'Mrs Sinkins'**, are very sweet-smelling. They are easy to grow, provided they have the right conditions, but you should accept that most will last only a few years before they need replanting.

Pinks are simply the modern cultivars of garden pinks. Many new cultivars appear all the time, most of which have a bushy habit of growth and striking flowers on long stalks, features which have sometimes been obtained at the expense of the scent. Good modern pinks include **'Doris'**, **'Ruby'**, **'Devon Pearl'** and **'Laetitia Wyatt'**. Laced pinks have rounded petals margined with the same colour as the centre of the flower; these plants are often very strongly scented. **'Laced Monarch'** and **'Gran's Favourite'** are good examples of this type.

PLANTING HELP Pinks do best in a sunny position in light, well-drained soil; they will not tolerate waterlogging. The older varieties grow well with little attention, whereas some of the modern varieties benefit from having their tips

Old garden pink 'Mrs Sinkins'

Malmaison carnation 'Old Blush'

Modern pink 'Doris'

Malmaison 'Blush Pink'

Malmaison carnation 'Thora'

pinched out, to encourage bushy growth. Hardy to −10°F (−23°C), US zones 6–10.

Malmaison Carnations

The best of all for scent, this group is descended from a carnation named **'Old Blush'** (syn. 'Souvenir de la Malmaison') raised in France in the 1850s. The name derives from the similarity of its flower to the rose also called 'Souvenir de la Malmaison'. At Malmaison, near Paris, was the house and garden belonging to Napoleon's wife, the Empress Josephine. Also illustrated here are **'Blush Pink'** and **'Thora'**. Hardy to 20°F (−6°C), US zones 9–10 .

PLANTING HELP   Malmaison carnations are not the easiest of plants to keep, and are usually grown in pots in peat or loam-based compost, and 'disbudded' (excess buds are removed) so that only 3–4 flower buds are left. They require partial shade and cool, airy conditions in the summer and greenhouse protection in winter, if they are to flower well.

Sweet William

Dianthus barbatus   A short-lived perennial often treated as a biennial that is native to S Europe, but has long been a popular cottage garden plant. Its strong stems, to about 2ft (60cm), make it an easy plant for the garden, as it needs no tying and staking, and it produces large flat heads of flowers throughout the summer. There are several varieties available commercially. Hardy to −10°F (−23°C), US zones 6–10.

PLANTING HELP   Sweet Williams are usually grown from seed, sown indoors in late spring, pricked out into trays and planted out into the garden in the autumn. They like a sunny position in well-drained but fertile soils.

Sweet Williams

'Gran's Favourite'

'Laced Monarch'

'Devon Pearl'

'Ruby'

'Laetitia Wyatt'

Garden pinks, flowering in early June

Lonicera etrusca at Spetchley Park, Worcestershire

Lonicera periclymenum 'Graham Thomas'

Honeysuckles

The climbing honeysuckles are the most useful of scented climbers for cool gardens. They are evergreen or deciduous woodland plants, twining through the undergrowth and flowering when they reach the sun in glades or on the tops of small trees. Honeysuckles come in various shades of cream, yellow, orange, pink or red and are often deliciously scented. It is worth noting that the American native wild red honeysuckles, such as *Lonicera sempervirens*, are brightly coloured and scentless and therefore have no place in this book.

PLANTING HELP   Honeysuckles should be planted in cool shade, in rich, moist, leafy soil where the plant can climb to the sun; a trellis or wall or an old apple tree make good supports. Ideally, the deciduous species should be planted in late autumn and the evergreen types in spring.

Common European Honeysuckle, Woodbine *Lonicera periclymenum*   This is the beautiful wild honeysuckle well known to country dwellers in Britain, where it is seen and smelled, rambling and scrambling through hedgerows from June to September. It is found wild throughout much of

Lonicera japonica 'Hall's Prolific'

Wild Common Honeysuckle

Lonicera periclymenum 'Belgica'

Europe and is naturalized in North America. It makes a deciduous shrub up to about 13ft (4m), with stems that become woody with age. It is well scented and has flowers opening cream and fading to yellow, tinged with red. Hardy to −20°F (−29°C), US zones 5–9.
'Graham Thomas' is an excellent cultivar with long-lasting, larger white flowers which turn yellow later. This plant was discovered by and named after the great British plantsman. Two older cultivars, **'Belgica'** and 'Serotina', so-called Early and Late Dutch, have red buds; they flower at slightly different times, but are otherwise very similar.

Japanese Honeysuckle *Lonicera japonica*
An equally well-scented climber, and more tolerant of dry conditions, it is also naturalized in North America, where it has grown so well that it has become a pest. The plant is a rampant ground-cover and climber with pairs of scented white to yellow flowers in the axils of the leaves. 'Halliana' is a good form, with flowers white at first, turning yellow later; **'Hall's Prolific'** is another good variety, with very strongly scented white, cream and yellow flowers; var. *repens* with purple stems and pink buds is a Chinese variety of *L. japonica*, and a third is 'Aureoreticulata' with gold-veined leaves. Hardy to −10°F (−23°C), US zones 6–9.

Lonicera etrusca A semi-evergreen shrubby climber that grows to 30ft (9m) with masses of rather small creamy yellow flowers around 1½in (4cm) long, in stalked whorls. Native to the

Mediterranean region, from Switzerland to Israel. One of the most floriferous of the honeysuckles, from midsummer onwards. Hardy to 0°F (−18°C), US zones 7–10.

Lonicera caprifolium A strong-growing deciduous honeysuckle that climbs to 10ft (3m), native to eastern Europe. The upper pairs of leaves join to form a cup, in which sits the stalkless whorl of flowers, to 2in (5cm) long. Hardy to −20°F (−29°C), US zones 5–9.

Lonicera caprifolium

Old Roses

Old roses are renowned for their good scent; was this because the only roses that survived were the well-scented ones, or because the early breeders happened to work with well-scented species? Certainly, two of the parents of the old pre-19th century roses, the Red rose *Rosa gallica* and the Musk rose *Rosa moschata*, are among the best-scented of all. These two, in various combinations, contributed their excellent scent to all the roses on these two pages.

PLANTING HELP   All roses are best planted from bare-rooted plants bought in winter. Be bold and trim the roots to 9in (23cm) or so, before planting in a good hole enriched with peat or leaf mould and a sprinkling of general fertilizer. Use farmyard manure as a mulch in spring when the plants are established. All these roses are hardy to −20°F (−29°C), US zones 5–10; a few are hardier.

Rosa '**Alba Maxima**'   A large arching shrub with a spread of 17ft (5m) and masses of white, double flowers around 3in (8cm) across. Flowering only in summer, for about a month in cool areas. Known at least since the 15th century. Hardy to −30°F (−35°C), US zones 4–8.

Rosa centifolia '**Muscosa**' The Old Moss Rose, Common Moss   This, the original mossy sport of *centifolia* was recorded in the late 17th century. It makes a lax shrub with a spread of 7ft (2m) and double pink flowers around 3½in (9cm) across. Its flower stems and sepals are well covered in moss.

It flowers once but over a long season of about two months.

Rosa '**Comte de Chambord**'   A Portland rose with upright stems to 5ft (1.5m), with large leaves and mid-pink, very double flowers around 3½in (9cm) across. Repeat-flowering in summer and again in autumn. Hardy to −30°F (−35°C), US zones 4–8.

Rosa × *damascena* '**Trigintipetala**' (syn. 'Kazanlik')   An ancient Damask, forming an upright bush that grows to 7ft (2m); flowers around 3in (8cm) across, rather loose double, with a wonderful scent. In places where it is grown for scent the plants are pruned with shears to around 3½ft (1m) high after flowering, and every five years or so cut to the ground. An ancient variety of unrecorded origin, but possibly *Rosa gallica* 'Officinalis' × *Rosa phoenicia*.

Rosa '**Mme Plantier**'   An Alba rose, possibly crossed with *Rosa moschata*, with upright stems that grow to 5ft (1.5m) or more if supported, with very double flowers opening cream from pink buds before turning to white, around 3in (8cm) across. Repeat-flowering in summer and again in autumn. Hardy to −30°F (−35 °C), US zones 4–8.

Rosa '**La Ville de Bruxelles**'   One of the largest-flowered and richest-coloured of the Damasks with fully double, flat flowers with a good scent, around 3½in (9cm) across. It forms a very leafy bush with stems to 5ft (1.5m). An altogether fine rose, but once-flowering only.

Rosa 'La Ville de Bruxelles'

Rosa centifolia 'Muscosa'

Rosa 'Mme Plantier' at Sissinghurst

Rosa 'Alba Maxima'

Rosa × *damascena* 'Trigintipetala' grown in order to produce Attar of Roses in Turkey

Rosa 'Comte de Chambord'

'The Countryman'

'Evelyn'

'St Swithun'

English Roses

This is a new group of roses which have been raised by David Austin in England since 1960. They combine the shapes, soft colours and good scents of the Old roses with the continuous flowering and disease-resistance of the new. The varieties on these two pages are especially recommended for their scent. Hardiness is generally to around −20°F (−29°C), US zones 5–9.

PLANTING HELP   These require the same planting care as the Old roses. Cut off the dead flowers as soon as the petals have dropped and shorten the shoots which have flowered by a third to prolong flowering. Feed and water throughout the summer.

'Brother Cadfael'   A very large-cupped but graceful flower of medium pink. Stems to 4ft (1.2m), rather upright. Introduced in 1990.

'Chianti'   The very dark red flowers, of medium size, are borne profusely, but only in summer. Stems to 5ft (1.5m), rather upright. Introduced in 1967. One of David Austin's early crosses between the almost black Gallica 'Tuscany' and the Floribunda 'Dusky Maiden'.

'Evelyn'   A large flat, fully double flower of medium apricot pink with a pale edge. Stems to 3½ft (1m), rather upright. Introduced in 1991. One of the strongest-scented of the English roses.

'Gertrude Jekyll'   A large flat, fully double flower of rich, dusky pink. Stems to 4ft (1.2m), rather upright. Another with very strong scent.

'Gertrude Jekyll'

'Jayne Austin'

'Chianti' at David Austin's nursery, at Albrighton, near Wolverhampton

A seedling of 'Comte de Chambord' introduced in 1986.

'Jayne Austin'   A cupped but graceful medium to large flower of soft yellow. Stems to 4ft (1.2m), rather upright. Scent like the yellow Tea roses. Introduced in 1990.

'St Swithun'   A shallow-cupped flower of soft pink, the edges later recurving. Stems to 3½ft (1m), strong and bushy. Scent very sweet. A seedling of the *Rosa rugosa* hybrid 'Conrad Ferdinand Meyer', introduced in 1993.

'The Countryman'   A very double flower, like an untidy rosette of deep pink. Stems to 3½ft (1m), strong and spreading. Scent very sweet. A seedling of 'Comte de Chambord' introduced in 1979.

'Brother Cadfael'

'Surpassing Beauty' in Eccleston Square, with a blue *Ceanothus*

'Surpassing Beauty'

'Fragrant Delight'

Hybrid Tea Roses

Most modern rose breeders have concentrated on breeding Hybrid Tea roses, aiming for large, striking flowers and regarding scent as less important. In spite of this, many newer roses still have a wonderful scent. Some of these, especially the climbers, have survived for many years and have now attained classic status themselves.

PLANTING HELP These need the same treatment as the English roses, but the bush forms need harder pruning in spring. Climbers need the new shoots tied in and the old wood removed in the winter or in cold climates, in spring. Most are hardy to −10°F (−23°C), US zones 6–9.

'Aloha' A large, pink-flowered Hybrid Tea with a superb scent. A large shrub or sometimes a small

'Radox Bouquet'

'Aloha'

climber to 10ft (3m), flowering repeatedly through the summer. Raised in the USA in 1949.

'Fragrant Delight' A Floribunda with medium-sized, rather loose flowers throughout the season and very shiny leaves. Stems to 4ft (1.2m). Raised in the USA in 1978.

'Guinée' A Hybrid Tea climber with medium-sized flowers of the deepest purplish red, with an excellent, heavy scent. Flowering mainly in summer, with a few later flowers. Raised in France in 1938.

'Ena Harkness'

'Ena Harkness' A lovely large, deep red Hybrid Tea rose, with petals rolled back at the edges, flowering freely throughout the season. The climbing form grows to 12ft (3.5m), the bush form to 5ft (1.5m). The bush raised in England in 1946.

'Radox Bouquet' A Floribunda with medium-sized, fully double flowers throughout the season, of a lovely pale pink with a darker centre. Stems to 4ft (1.2m). Raised in England in 1981.

'Surpassing Beauty' An old climbing Hybrid Tea, found by the rosarian Humphrey Brooke at Wolverstone Church, Suffolk. A climber to 8ft (2.5m), repeat-flowering with an excellent scent.

'Guinée'

Hoya carnosa

Hoya

Hoyas are tender climbing shrubs from Asia, Polynesia and Australia. They do not need full sun and, if grown in pots, are useful plants to bring into the house from the greenhouse when in flower in order to enjoy their superb scent.

Hoya carnosa   A shrubby climber that grows to 20ft (6m) or more with very thick, oval, waxy leaves to 3in (8cm) long. In summer it produces tight rounded umbels of pink flowers to 3in (8cm) across, which look as if they are made of icing sugar. One flower head will scent a room. Native to China and southern Japan, growing over rocks like ivy. Hardy to 32°F (0°C), US zone 10.

PLANTING HELP   Put the young plant in a pot of loose, leafy soil and keep on the dry side in winter, water more in summer. Grows well in deep shade, but needs some sun to flower freely. Do not cut off the old flower stalks, as they will continue to produce more flowers for years.

Hoya lanceolata subsp. ***bella***   A spreading and hanging sub-shrub that grows to 18in (45cm), with waxy pointed leaves to 1¼in (3cm) long. It produces small, flat umbels of white flowers with a purple centre, around 2in (5cm) across, in late summer, with the scent of stephanotis. Native to the Himalayas. Hardy to 32°F (0°C), US zone 10.

PLANTING HELP   A good plant for a hanging basket in the greenhouse; warm and moist in summer, drier and cooler in winter.

Dregea

Dregea sinensis (syn. *Wattakaka sinensis*) Like a hardier *Hoya*, with climbing and twining stems that grow to 6ft (1.8m) or more. The thin, heart-shaped, pointed leaves are deciduous. The umbels of scented pink flowers with white centres are produced in succession through the summer. Hardy to 0°F (−18°C), US zones 7–10.

PLANTING HELP   A tough climber for a wall or to clamber into a shrub, in sun or a little shade. Any good soil, moist in summer.

Stephanotis

Stephanotis floribunda Madagascar Jasmine A tropical climber that grows to 15ft (4.5m) or more, native to Madagascar, with thin, waxy, oval leaves to 4in (10cm) long. The tubular, waxy white flowers, to 2in (5cm) long, with a wonderfully sweet, exotic scent, are produced in summer or

Hoya lanceolata subsp. *bella* in a hanging basket

Dregea sinensis growing wild in Sichuan, China

Gardenia augusta wild form in Hong Kong

Gardenia *Gardenia augusta* 'Veitchiana'

6 weeks after the beginning of the rains. Needs temperatures above 60°F (15°C), US zone 11.

PLANTING HELP   Not easy to grow outside the tropics, needing ample heat and humidity to grow and flower satisfactorily.

Gardenia

Gardenia *Gardenia augusta* 'Veitchiana' (syn. *Gardenia jasminoides*, *G. florida*)   In the early 20th century no elegant gentleman's evening dress was complete without a gardenia in his buttonhole. It is an evergreen shrub that grows to 5ft (1.5m) tall with shiny leaves and heavily scented, double white flowers around 2in (5cm) across. The single-flowered wild form is native to China, and is found on Victoria Peak, Hong Kong. Hardy to 20°F (−6°C), US zones 9–10.

PLANTING HELP   Needs acid soil and ample heat and humidity in summer, with cooler, drier conditions in winter. During dry periods, spray regularly with rainwater.

Stephanotis floribunda

Sweet peas growing on twigs at the back of a border at Hampton Court

Sweet Peas

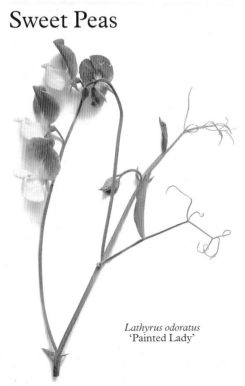

Lathyrus odoratus
'Painted Lady'

There are more than 100 annual and perennial species of the genus *Lathyrus*, but when we talk about sweet peas we refer to the well-known large-flowered cultivars which are derived from *Lathyrus odoratus*, an attractive, scented, small-flowered annual species which is itself well worth growing (*see below*).

Sweet peas were bred and grown in huge quantities in Victorian times as cut flowers and their popularity was given another boost in the early years of this century by the arrival of the larger, wavy-edged 'Spencer' types, named after Countess Spencer of Althrop. These Spencer types have been steadily improved, giving rise to the sweet peas commonly sold and grown today. There are hundreds of different named varieties, including dwarfs, and new introductions are appearing all the time. Nearly all are scented, some with outstanding scent. Hardy to 20°F (–6°C), US zones 9–10.

PLANTING HELP   Sweet peas are easy to grow from seed, sown either indoors in early autumn or early spring, or directly outdoors once the soil has begun to warm up. If sowing indoors, place the seed in moist seed or potting compost in a tray or pot, at a depth of about ½in (1.5cm). To encourage germination, keep the seeds in a frost-free greenhouse or on a windowsill in a cool room. Water after sowing, but do not water again until

Old varieties of sweet pea in the kitchen garden at Heligan, Cornwall

the seedlings have emerged, and then only sparingly. Once they have germinated, the seedlings require plenty of light and ventilation; the ideal place is a cold frame or under a cloche.

To obtain good bushy plants and plenty of flowers, pinch out the growing tips, leaving only two pairs of leaves, to encourage the formation of side shoots. Plant out in good soil in a sunny, sheltered place once the weather improves. Provide some kind of support – a fence, trellis or wigwam of canes, preferably covered with wire or mesh. It is important to cut sweet peas regularly, for once a plant has begun to form seed pods, it will stop producing flowers.

Lathyrus odoratus The wild sweet pea is an annual climber, probably native to S Italy, Sicily and some of the Greek Islands. It grows up to 7ft (2m) tall with small green leaflets arranged in pairs and typical pea flowers to about 1in (2.5cm) across, highly scented, purple in the wild, but varying in colour in cultivation. The variety **'Cupani'** is one of the closest to the wild type; **'Painted Lady'** has been known since 1726.

Old-fashioned sweet peas 'Cupani'

Flowering Tobacco *Nicotiana*

Nicotiana 'Domino Salmon Pink'

Tobacco *Nicotiana tabacum*

Tobacco Plants

There are over 60 species and many hybrids of annual and perennial *Nicotiana*, some of which are grown commercially for smoking. *Nicotiana* is much admired by gardeners for its attractive, sweetly scented flowers, which usually open in the evening. Hardy to about 32°F (0°C), US zone 10.

PLANTING HELP   Most ornamental tobaccos like a warm, sunny position in rich, well-drained soil. They are easy to grow from seed sown indoors in early spring and planted out once the weather has warmed up. Those listed below are perennial, but are treated as annuals in the Northern Hemisphere; in exceptionally mild winters they may seed themselves. The taller varieties may require staking in exposed places. **Note:** tobacco plants are poisonous, as they contain nicotine.

Flowering Tobacco *Nicotiana alata* (syn. *N. affinis*)   A native of South America, this rather tender perennial is usually grown as an annual. It reaches about 5ft (1.5m) tall, with upright branches bearing soft leaves, sticky to the touch, and long tubular flowers along the stems from June to September. Each flower is about 3in (8cm) long, greenish white on the outside and white on the inside. The flowers are very fragrant in the evening, but will also open during the day in dull, cloudy weather. *Nicotiana alata* has given rise to many named garden hybrids with different coloured flowers, and new ones appear all the time. Among them are **'Evening Fragrance'**, mixed colours, and **'Fragrant Cloud'** and **'Domino Salmon Pink'** which produce flowers of one colour.

Nicotiana sylvestris   This is a sturdy perennial with thick roots and stout branched stems up to 6ft (1.8m) tall. The large green leaves are more or less elliptic in shape, to about 2ft (60cm) long and thin and delicate in texture. Loose heads of scented, white funnel-shaped flowers appear in August; they close in bright sun, but will open on dull days. Native to Argentina. Hardy to 20°F (–6°C), US zones 9–10 for short periods only. The roots will sprout in spring if protected from frost.

Tobacco *Nicotiana tabacum*   Native to South America, this annual or biennial species is grown as commercial tobacco. It is a large plant, to 6ft (1.8m) or more tall, with huge leaves that are about 2ft (60cm) long. Loose clusters of greenish white or pink funnel-shaped flowers, each to about 3in (8cm) long, appear in August, and, unlike some of the other species, will stay open even in

Nicotiana 'Fragrant Cloud'

Nicotiana 'Evening Fragrance'

Nicotiana sylvestris

bright sunlight. 'Variegata' is a shorter form with smaller cream and green variegated leaves (*not illustrated here*). Hardy to 20°F (–6°C), US zones 9–10 for short periods only.

Petunias

Petunias are closely related to the tobaccos, and have flowers of basically similar shape; in both groups, the white or cream flowers are the most heavily scented. There are about 35 species of *Petunia* native to tropical South America and large numbers of named hybrids. Some species are annual, others perennial, but the hybrids from the perennial types are tender and are therefore treated as annuals. Hardy to 20°F (–6°C), US zones 9–10 for short periods only.

PLANTING HELP   Petunias are usually grown annually from seed sown indoors during late winter and early spring, and planted out once the danger of frost has passed. The seed requires a temperature of about 60°F (15 °C) to germinate. The perennial trailing Surfinia varieties, often sold as young plants, are particularly suitable for large containers, as they can trail over the edge; they come in definite colours, usually purple or white. Water carefully and keep dead-heading to prolong the flowering.

Petunia 'Prime Time White' with *Impatiens*

Madonna Lily *Lilium candidum*

A large pot of 'Star Gazer' in a Clapham garden

Lilium

There are about 100 species of *Lilium* and numerous hybrids, some of which are scented, some not. There are many different shapes, sizes and colours of flower, ranging from the simple trumpet-shapes to the 'Turks-cap' types. All are grown from bulbs, which are best bought from a specialist nursery.

PLANTING HELP   Lilies have a reputation for being difficult to grow, and while this is true of some species, the easier varieties shown here should be easy to grow well. Be on guard against slugs, which devour lily shoots whenever they appear, and either scatter slug pellets liberally or make a 'slug pub' (a jar of beer dregs sunk into the ground, which will trap large numbers of the pests). Buy only firm, plump-looking bulbs from a good source in October, and start them in pots (safer from slugs) with chippings in the base below them to provide good drainage, and a good, loose compost above. Plant the bulbs deeply, although this does not apply to *L. candidum* (which should be shallow), and water sparingly, increasing the amount once the plants are in bud. Place the lilies near a seat so that you can enjoy the scent, and once you've successfully reared a pot of lilies you will feel confident enough to grow them in the garden, where they will make a wonderful display during the early summer.

Madonna Lily *Lilium candidum*   Native to the eastern Mediterranean region, where it grows in rocky places and flowers in May, this well-known cottage garden plant does best in well-drained chalky soil with plenty of well-rotted manure added. The lowest leaves usually appear in the autumn and remain green throughout the winter. Hardy to 0°F (−18°C), US zones 7–10 or less.

Lilium regale   One of the easiest lilies to grow and one of the most popular, this species is native to western China where it flowers in summer. Stems grow to about 7ft (2m) and are scattered with narrow green leaves, topped with spectacular

A group of *Lilium regale* in a large pot

clusters of white, trumpet-shaped flowers, flushed pink on the outside and yellow on the inside. This lily needs limy soils and likes a sunny position in the garden. It does best when its young shoots are protected from late frosts. Hardy to −20°F (−29°C), US zones 5–9.

Lilium monadelphum (syn. *Lilium szovitzianum*)   A native of the Caucasus mountains, where we have seen it growing in great drifts on steep grassy meadows. This spectacular lily grows up to 6ft (1.8m) tall and produces clusters of large, pendulous, golden yellow flowers, sometimes finely spotted with orange, from June to August. It does best in good garden soil, and once established, should last for many years. Hardy to −10°F (−23°C), US zones 6–9.

Golden-rayed lily of Japan *Lilium auratum*
A subtropical lily with glossy leaves and wide-open white flowers with a yellow central stripe. Native to Japan where it grows in warm, volcanic soils. Stems of varying height, up to 6ft (1.8m) with as many as 10 flowers, 5–9in (12–23cm) across. A good plant for a pot in well-drained, sandy soil, flowering in summer and autumn. Easily grown outside in warm areas. Hardy to 20°F (−6°C), US zones 9–10.

***Lilium* 'Star Gazer'**   A hybrid of *Lilium auratum* with upright flowers flushed with crimson pink. A good plant for a large pot with excellently scented flowers, which last well. Keep almost dry in winter. Hardy to 20°F (−6°C), US zones 9–10.

Lilium monadelphum wild in the Caucasus

Golden-rayed lily of Japan *Lilium auratum*

Arum Lily at Trebah, Cornwall

Giant Lily at Inverewe, Scotland

Arum Lily

Zantedeschia aethiopica An herbaceous perennial with a large tuberous root, green leaves and a pure white spathe curled around a yellow spike, called a spadix. This is a very common plant in South Africa, growing in wet fields and shallow water, flowering in early spring. Leaf and flower stems grow to 5ft (1.5m). Flowers delicately scented. Look out for *Z. odorata*, a newly described species, which smells strongly of freesias. Hardy to 20° F (–6°C), US zones 9–10.

PLANTING HELP When in growth, give the plants rich soil, ample water and warmth. They will tolerate a little frost while dormant.

Giant Lily

Cardiocrinum giganteum (syn. *Lilium giganteum*) A native to the Himalayas where it grows in wet forests and scrub, this huge plant has stems up to 13ft (4m) tall, clothed lower down with broad green leaves. The beautiful trumpet-shaped flowers, which appear in June and July, are white with a central dark red blotch and have a fine scent which is carried on the air. Hardy to 0°F (–18°C), US zones 7–10 or less if the bulbs are protected by a deep, loose mulch.

PLANTING HELP This is easily grown from bulbs. It needs a rich, moist, but well-drained soil with plenty of leaf mould, a shady place and protection from slugs, which love the young shoots, leaves and seed pods. *Cardiocrinum* looks at its most natural in a woodland setting and is best planted on a slope to prevent the bulbs becoming waterlogged. The young leaves will need to be protected from late frosts, which can be done by covering the young shoots on frosty nights.

Gladiolus

Gladiolus murielae (syn. *Gladiolus callianthus*, *Acidanthera bicolor*) This is one of the best-scented and easiest of the *Gladiolus*, of which there are over 170 species. Native to East Africa, where it grows on wet rock ledges and grassy places, flowering in summer. The tall stems grow to 3½ft (1m) and carry up to 5 long-tubed, lily-scented flowers to 6in (15cm) long, white with a purple blotch near the base of the petals. Hardy to 32°F (0°C), US zone 10.

PLANTING HELP Plant the corms in late spring in rich soil and keep well watered until flowering has finished. Lift the plants before the arrival of penetrating frost and store dry indoors. Outside keep dry in winter, water in summer.

Freesias grown in a pot indoors

Gladiolus murielae on Zomba Mountain, Malawi

Freesia

These are among the best scented of all bulbs.
Wild *Freesia corymbosa*, which is native to the
Cape Province of South Africa, may have yellow,
white, or rarely, pinkish flowers, but modern
varieties have a wider range of colours and much
larger flowers, but less scent. In general the yellow
or white-flowered ones are the best scented. Stems
to 2ft (60cm); flowers 2in (5cm) across. Hardy to
20°F (–6°C), US zones 9–10.

PLANTING HELP   Easily grown from corms
in sandy, rich soil. Water and feed while in growth,
then keep dry and warm as the leaves go yellow,
before starting again in spring. Good outdoors in
California.

Hymenocallis

Hymenocallis × festalis (syn. *Ismene × festalis*)
A large bulb with deciduous leaves and umbels of
few sweetly scented white flowers, a cross between
H. narcissiflora and *H. longipetala* from Peru,
Ecuador and Bolivia, flowering mainly in early
summer in gardens. The stem grows to 4ft (1.2m)
and carries around 4 flowers, each with a long
tube and narrow, arching lobes; corona with 6
feathery lobes between the short stamens. Leaves
are 12–18in (30–45cm) long. Hardy to 32°F (0°C),
US zone 10.

PLANTING HELP   Plant the bulbs in late
spring in rich soil, keeping them warm and humid
in summer, and dry and warm in winter.

Mixed freesia

Hymenocallis × festalis

71

Primula anisodora in Devon

Primula florindae by a burn at Littlewood Park, Scotland

Primulas

Although there are about 500 different species of *Primula*, it is obvious that we can include only two or three in a book this size. Many are scented, including some of those which can be grown as pot plants, but here we mention a couple for growing outside. Hardy to 0°F (−18°C), US zones 7–10 or less.

PLANTING HELP   Easy to grow in wet soil in shade or partial shade.

Giant Cowslip *Primula florindae*   One of the largest primulas, the Giant Cowslip grows up to about 3ft (90cm), with clusters of pale yellow, bell-like flowers from June to August. It is native to southeast Tibet and southwest China, where it grows in shady bogs and along streams. Some forms have orange to reddish orange flowers.

Primula anisodora   A hardy clump-forming perennial with stems that grow to 2ft (60cm), carrying whorls of nodding, very dark maroon red flowers with a sweet scent. Native to western China in Yunnan and Sichuan.

Cherry Pie

Heliotrope *Heliotropium arborescens*   There are about 250 species of *Heliotropium*, most of which are rather tender shrubs or annuals. The species illustrated here is native to Peru and is well known to gardeners. In the wild it makes a shrub that grows to 7ft (2m) tall, while the many named forms and hybrids in cultivation are much shorter than this. In temperate gardens this plant is often bedded out to provide a display of colour throughout the summer. When grown as a pot plant, it will normally reach 1ft (30cm), but in a greenhouse it can be considerably larger. The rather wrinkled leaves are darkish green and the tiny scented flowers are borne in clusters to around 3in (8cm) across. The flower colour varies from white to lilac or dark purple in the form **'Marine'**. Hardy to 32°F (0°C), US zone 10.

PLANTING HELP   Cherry Pie is normally treated as an annual or half-hardy perennial, planted outside, either in the border or in a pot, once the danger of frost has passed. It is also very effective as a plant for a cool conservatory, where its scent can be appreciated at close quarters. Cherry Pie can be grown from seed sown indoors in early spring or from small plants obtained from a nursery. It does best in good moist, but well-drained soil in sun or partial shade, and should be watered freely during the growing season. Large plants grown as standard specimens outside can be dug up, brought into the greenhouse and potted up for the winter.

Cosmos

Cosmos atrosanguineus   There are more than 20 species of *Cosmos* but *Cosmos atrosanguineus* is the only well-scented one. This perennial species is native to Mexico, but is now apparently rare in the wild and is seen more frequently in gardens. It grows to 3½ft (1m), flowering in summer and autumn. Each flower is around 2½in (6cm) across with about 8 velvety maroon petals, smelling surprisingly of dark chocolate. Hardy to 20°F (−6°C), US zones 9–10.

Heliotrope *Heliotropium arborescens* 'Marine'

Phlox 'Silver Salmon', a good rich pink

PLANTING HELP   *Cosmos atrosanguineus* is grown from tubers, which do best in a warm sunny place in moist, but well-drained soil. They need to be treated much like dahlias – in areas where long periods of frost are expected, the young tubers should be dug up and stored in a frost-free place, before replanting in spring. As they get older, the tubers will become more frost-resistant and they will survive outside if covered with a thick layer of straw, bracken or fleece and possibly a cloche or dome, which will also protect the roots from waterlogging.

Phlox

Phlox paniculata   There are over 60 species of phlox, some annual, some perennial, all of them native to America. *Phlox paniculata* is suitable for the herbaceous border, with its strong stems and attractive, scented flowers from July to September. It grows to about 3ft (90cm) tall, with narrow green leaves and dense heads of simple little flowers, often with an eye of a contrasting colour. These can range from white and pink through to lilac and purple, and there are many named varieties available, some of them shorter and more robust than the original species. Hardy to −10°F (−23°C), US zones 6–9.

PLANTING HELP   Phlox does best in deep, moist, rich soils in sun or dappled shade. It is not very long-lived, tending to deteriorate after five or six years, but you can help by providing a mulch of good, well-rotted manure in spring and cutting out any feeble stems. To perpetuate your stock, dig up a plant in early spring and pull it gently apart before replanting.

Phlox paniculata 'Fujiyama', a fine large white form

The chocolate-scented *Cosmos atrosanguineus*

Jasminum azoricum

Spanish Jasmine *Jasminum grandiflorum*

Jasmines

Jasminum is a very large genus of about 200 evergreen or upright shrubs and woody climbers, native to the tropical and temperate regions of the Old World and Australia, with one species in America. Jasmines can be planted in borders, clipped to form hedges or trained up trelliswork or another host plant. Most of them make excellent conservatory plants.

PLANTING HELP   Plant outdoor or hardier varieties of jasmine in well-drained but moisture-retentive soil in sheltered, sunny sites where possible. Frost-tender species do well in pots in a cool greenhouse or conservatory in fertile, loam-based soil with wires for support. Water regularly in summer, sparingly in winter; make sure they are well ventilated. Red spider mite and scale insect are frequent pests. Most species do not require much pruning but overgrown plants should be thinned as needed. Spanish Jasmine (*see next entry*) is commonly sold as pots of around 5 rooted cuttings, 8in (20cm) tall, in flower in late autumn. To keep the plants for future years, carefully repot in sandy loam as soon as possible and keep on the dry side through the winter, in the greenhouse in cold areas, in full light. *J. polyanthum* (*see page 14*) is sold in pots at Christmas.

Spanish Jasmine 'de Grasse' *Jasminum grandiflorum*   A lax or scrambling evergreen shrub that grows to 10ft (3m) and flowers in summer and autumn. The leathery leaves usually have 7 leaflets; the strongly scented white flowers have a tube just under ¾in (2cm) long and lobes almost as long, reddish outside when grown in full light. A shrub of uncertain origin, but long cultivated by the Moors in Spain; from there it spread to S Europe. Easily grown in dry, warm areas. Hardy to 20°F (−6°C), US zones 9–10.

***Jasminum officinale* 'Affine'** (syn. *Jasminum officinale* 'Grandiflorum')   The large-flowered form of the deciduous and hardy common jasmine is native to the Himalayas. A twining climber that grows to 20ft (6m) with long pointed leaflets and flowers to 1¼in (3cm) long, flushed reddish outside. Hardy to 10°F (−12°C), US zones 8–10. Easily grown on a warm wall or fence in hot areas.

Jasminum azoricum   A scrambling shrub native to Madeira, flowering much of the year. It grows to 20ft (6m) with shiny 3-foliolate leaves and scented white flowers. Twigs rounded. Flowers around 1in (2.5cm) across, with 5–6 narrow lobes in terminal bunches of around 9. Hardy to 20°F (−6°C), US zones 9–10. Easily grown on a warm wall or scrambling into shrubs.

Sambac Arabian Jasmine *Jasminum sambac*
A spreading shrub native to India, Burma and Sri
Lanka, flowering for much of the year. It grows to
10ft (3m), with simple, broad leaves to 5in (12cm)
long and a tight terminal head of heavily scented,
white flowers around 1in (2.5cm) across, with 7
wide lobes. This is the jasmine which is sacred to
Vishnu and is used to flavour jasmine tea. **'Maid
of Orleans'** has large single flowers and in
'Grand Duke of Tuscany' (syn. 'Flore Pleno')
the flowers are double. Best above 60°F (15°C),
US zone 11. Needs a warm climate such as Hawaii
to thrive outdoors or ample warmth and humidity
in a greenhouse.

Jasminum officinale 'Affine'

Jasminum humile **'Revolutum'**
A semi-evergreen shrub that grows to 8ft (2.5m)
across, with green stems and yellow waxy flowers
1in (2.5cm) across. This is the largest-flowered and
best-scented clone of *J. humile*. It is easily grown
in a warm position. Hardy to 20°F (−6°C),
US zones 9–10.

Star Jasmine

Trachelospermum jasminoides   A jasmine-
like evergreen climbing shrub that grows to 10ft
(3m) or more, with simple leaves and scented,
white to pale yellow jasmine-like flowers 1in
(2.5cm) across. Native to S China, Vietnam,
S Japan and Korea, where it climbs on trees in the
forest, flowering in April–May. Fruit long, narrow
and bean-like, pinkish red. Hardy to 10°F
(−12°C), US zones 8–10.

PLANTING HELP   An attractive plant for a
large pot, pruned as a shrub and brought
undercover in winter.

Jasminum sambac 'Maid of Orleans'

Jasminum sambac 'Grand Duke of Tuscany'

Star Jasmine *Trachelospermum jasminoides*

Jasminum humile 'Revolutum'

Bay in flower

Bay

Laurus nobilis   The bay is a noble evergreen
tree, native to the Mediterranean region, although
long cultivated elsewhere. It is worth growing for
its aromatic evergreen foliage and attractive
appearance and can be allowed to grow up
naturally or clipped into a formal shape. Although
bay can eventually grow up to about 65ft (20m)
tall, it is more commonly seen in gardens as a
trimmed bush of about 7–10ft (2–3m). In very
cold weather it may be cut right back by frost, but
will often sprout up again the following spring.
The glossy green leaves give off a wonderful smell
when crushed and insignificant greenish yellow
flowers appear during late summer. Hardy down
to about 20°F (–6°C), US zones 9–10. The leaves
are useful both for pot pourri and in cooking, and
can be used fresh throughout the year, but have a
more pronounced flavour when dried.

PLANTING HELP   It is really worth buying a
bay tree from a good tree or shrub nursery; they
are usually expensive, but you need only get a
small one and it should live for years. Bay is easy
to grow, preferring a well-drained but moisture-
retentive soil and a sunny position; once
established it is very tolerant of drought; it can
also be grown in pots, but make sure there is room
for growth.

Lemon Balm

Melissa officinalis   Lemon Balm, sometimes
called Bee Balm is a perennial native to southern
Europe, but naturalized in Britain and parts of
North America. It makes a bush up to about 2ft
(60cm) tall and produces small whitish yellow
flowers during the summer and early autumn. The
leaves have a delicate lemon scent and can be
dried and used as tea or in pot pourri. Hardy to
–10°F (–23°C), US zones 6–9 or less. *M. officinalis*
'Aurea' has green leaves variegated with cream.

PLANTING HELP   Lemon Balm will usually
grow well in almost any soil, in sun or shade. It can
be invasive, as it spreads by means of a creeping
woody rootstock, but it is nevertheless a good,
tough plant for a spot at the edge of a path where
it can be brushed against.

Mint

There are about 25 species and many varieties of
mint, most of which originate from Asia and
southern Europe. Although they are probably best
known for their culinary use, a number of them
have beautiful flowers too.

Clipped bay at Cranbourne Manor in Dorset

PLANTING HELP   Most mints are creeping plants which will spread freely if given the chance, so they are best restrained by planting in a confined spot next to a wall or path. They prefer rich soil in part shade where the soil will not dry out too quickly. Mints tend to deteriorate after a few years, but they are easy to propagate by pulling off rooted runners and replanting.

Corsican Mint *Mentha requienii* This creeping mint forms mats of tiny bright green leaves, which give off a delightful peppermint smell when crushed, so it is good for growing in cracks in paths. The minute lilac flowers appear throughout the summer. Hardy to 0°F (−18°C), US zones 7–10.

Corsican Mint

Eau de Cologne Mint *Mentha × piperita* 'Citrata' This grows to about 2ft (60cm) and has smooth-stalked, slightly bronze purplish green leaves that smell rather like Eau de Cologne, and small clusters of lilac purple flowers. An invasive variety, this sends out purple runners both below and above the ground. The aromatic qualities of this plant are most pronounced if grown in a sunny spot, but it also needs moisture. This mint has a better scent than taste. Hardy to −30°F (−35°C), US zones 4–8.

Wild Marjoram

Origanum vulgare A woody perennial herb native from Europe, including Britain, to western China, where it grows on limestone hills and chalk downland. It normally grows to about 2ft (60cm) or more tall and has pinkish purple flowers throughout the late summer. It is very variable and there are other forms with pink or white flowers (*not shown here*); there are also many other ornamental species and hybrids grown chiefly for their showy flowers or coloured bracts. In addition to its aromatic scent, marjoram will also attract bees and butterflies to your garden. Hardy to 0°F (−18°C), US zones 7–10.

PLANTING HELP
All *Origanums* like well-drained, dry soil in full sun; a raised bed is perfect for them. Wild marjoram can be grown from the very fine seed, sown in spring in compost that is kept only slightly moist; if you have a heated tray which will provide bottom heat, use it. Pot up the seedlings once they are big enough to handle and plant out once the soil has warmed up.

Wild Marjoram

Young leaves of Eau de Cologne Mint

Melissa officinalis 'Aurea'

Lemon Verbena *Aloysia triphylla*

Lemon Verbena

Aloysia triphylla (syn. *Lippia citriodora*)
A rather tender deciduous shrub native to Chile.
It grows up to about 16ft (4.5m) tall and is popular
as a long-lived plant for the conservatory or cool
greenhouse, where the delicious lemon scent is
incredibly powerful. The long, fairly narrow, pale
green leaves are the source of the scent, the tiny,
pale mauve flowers being attractive, but rather
insignificant. Hardy to 20°F (–6°C), US zones
9–10. The leaves dry extremely well and are a good
addition to pot pourri.

PLANTING HELP   Lemon verbena needs a
warm sunny position in well-drained soil. In mild
climates, such as southern California and the
south coast of England, it can be grown outside
satisfactorily, although the protection of a warm
wall should be provided. In areas where
temperatures regularly fall below freezing it is
better either grown in a pot and brought in for the
winter, or else grown as a permanent conservatory
plant. If it is to stay out during the winter, wrap it
in fleece or straw.

Prostanthera

Prostanthera cuneata   A rather tender
evergreen shrub native to southern Australia and
Tasmania, where it flowers in the summer. It
grows to about 3ft (90cm) and has tiny, glossy
green leaves which emit a powerful minty smell
when brushed past. The small white flowers, with
purple blotches in the throat, are also attractive.
Hardy to 20°F (–6°C), US zones 9–10.

PLANTING HELP   Will do best in moist, but
well-drained soil, in a sunny position.

Prostanthera cuneata

Catmints & Calamints

There are about 250 different species of catmints,
native to Europe and parts of Asia but also
naturalized in North America and Japan. All
prefer well-drained soil in a sunny position, which
is why they are excellent plants for the front of a
border or alongside a path. They have scented
foliage which gives off its fragrance when you
brush against it. They flower in summer over a
long period.

PLANTING HELP   Catmint and calamint are
related and both need well-drained soil in a sunny
position; they will tolerate poor soil, but if given
more fertile conditions growth will be more
luxuriant, sometimes at the expense of the flowers.
Both will also tolerate partial shade, but neither

Lesser Calamint *Calamintha nepeta* subsp. *nepeta*

Wild Catmint *Nepeta cataria*

Nepeta × faasseniia hedge

will survive waterlogging, especially in winter, so provide a well-drained site. Catmint looks particularly good grown as a low hedge on a bank, giving a hazy blue and grey effect. If possible, trim the plants thoroughly after flowering to encourage a second flush later in the season, and to prevent the plants from becoming too sprawling. Cuttings usually do well and should be taken from the non-flowering young shoot tips during early summer.

Catmint or **Catnip** *Nepeta cataria*
An herbaceous perennial originally used as a medicinal and culinary herb. It grows up to about 3½ft (1m) tall, in dry, grassy or scrubby places and has greyish green, strongly aromatic leaves, beloved of all members of the cat tribe. The small white flowers with bluish spots are in dense spikes and appear during midsummer. Hardy to −30°F (−35°C), US zones 4–8.

Nepeta × faassenii This is also confusingly known as catmint, but has greyish leaves and lavender blue flowers. It is low-growing, to 1ft (30cm), and if kept well trimmed, is useful as an edging plant for hot dry borders or paths, producing several flushes of flowers throughout the season. **'Six Hills Giant'** is a taller and more robust version, with deep blue flowers and stems up to 3½ft (1m). There are also many other named forms, with flowers in shades of white, lilac and blue. Hardy to −30°F (−35°C), US zones 4–8.

Calamint *Calamintha grandiflora* This is native to southern Europe where it grows in woodland

and scrub. It does well in any good soil in sun or partial shade. It grows to about 2ft (60cm) tall and has small pale green leaves, which are aromatic when crushed, and very attractive bright pink, sage-like flowers from June–October. Hardy to 0°F (−18°C), US zones 7–10.

Lesser Calamint *Calamintha nepeta* subsp. *nepeta* (syn. *C. nepetioides*) An aromatic perennial native to Europe and North Africa, that grows to 2ft (60cm) tall with leaves smelling strongly of mint when crushed. The small lilac or white flowers are carried from June–October, and so are especially valuable for their late flowering and are much visited by bees. 'White Cloud' and 'Blue Cloud' are selections with flowers of the two colours. Hardy to 0°F (−18°C), US zones 7–10.

Calamint *Calamintha grandiflora*

Artemisia 'Powis Castle' at Powis Castle

Curry Plant *Helichrysum italicum*

Aromatic Shrubs

Most of the shrubs shown on these pages are native to the Mediterranean region and have scented leaves which help to protect them from grazing animals. They are adapted to poor, stony hillsides and a climate with cool wet winters and hot, dry summers. Most are hardy for short periods to 10°F (−12°C), US zones 8–10.

PLANTING HELP   All the plants on this page will grow outside in the warmer parts of western Europe, as far north as Scotland, but may be killed in unusually severe winters. In California they do very well and can survive without irrigation in summer once they are established.

Ozothamnus

Ozothamnus ledifolius   A dense evergreen shrub that grows to 4ft (1.2m) tall, with small leaves covered in sticky aromatic gum and masses of small white flowers from pink buds. A native of Tasmania, where it grows in the mountains. Its scent hangs on the air in warm, moist weather. For any good soil, with some water in summer in dry areas.

Myrtle

Myrtus communis   A large evergreen shrub or small tree native to the Mediterranean region, that grows to 12ft (3.5m) with aromatic leathery leaves to 1in (2.5cm) long. The small creamy white flowers, around 1in (2.5cm) across, with a fluffy mass of stamens, are produced in summer, followed by juicy purplish black fruit. The variety *tarentina* has thicker, narrower leaves and is a little hardier. Both need protection from freezing wind.

Myrtle

Cistus ladanifer in southwest Spain

Cistus

Cistus ladanifer A shrub native to dry hills in SW Spain, Portugal, S France and North Africa. It grows to 6ft (1.8m) with sticky leaves and a succession of white flowers 2–4in (5–10cm) across, usually with a purple spot on each petal. The large flowers and narrow sticky leaves are characteristic of this species. The scented leaves of many *Cistus* species and hybrids can be smelled best in warm and humid or very hot weather.

Artemisia

Artemisia 'Powis Castle' A softly hairy, silvery shrub that grows to 5ft (1.5m) tall and wide, of uncertain origin but probably a seedling of *Artemisia arborescens* from the Mediterranean region, which appeared at Powis Castle in Wales. Flowers are very rarely produced and the leaves, with narrow lobes, are strongly scented when rubbed. The plants can be pruned quite hard in late spring if they become too straggly. Propagation is easiest by layering, though cuttings can be slow to root.

Artemisia 'Powis Castle'

Curry Plant

Helichrysum italicum A silvery sub-shrub with narrow leaves smelling strongly of curry when crushed. Its flowers are insignificant and small, in a head on a longish stalk to 1ft (30cm). Old plants are usually less than 3½ft (1m) in diameter.

Ozothamnus ledifolius

Buddleja davidii

Buddleja davidii 'Dartmoor'

Clethra arborea

Buddleja

***Buddleja davidii* and varieties**   These are very common shrubs, but are still among the best for their honey-scented flowers which attract butterflies. Colours range from very dark blue, purple, reddish purple and pinkish to pure white. It has been my impression that butterflies prefer the white form to the other colours. *B. davidii* is native to western China where it grows in disturbed places and on the shingly banks of rivers. Hardy to 10°F (−12°C), US zones 8–10. Other similar varieties of *Buddleja* are more refined and equally well-scented. **'Dartmoor'** has branched heads of purplish flowers on a slenderer bush; 'Lochinch' has slender, greyish leaves and pale blue flowers; it is my favourite and will flower well a second time if the first flowers are removed.

PLANTING HELP   Easily grown in well-drained soil in full sun. Wild seedlings will tend to be a nondescript colour, so to get a purple or white you will need to buy named plants.

Clerodendrum

A large genus of trees and shrubs, mainly from Africa and Asia, only a few of which are cultivated in gardens; the majority are tender and not suitable for growing outdoors. The two we show have fetid leaves and scented flowers.

PLANTING HELP   Easily grown in any soil in sun or partial shade from rooted suckers. Plant where you will not brush against the leaves which give off a strong pungent odour.

Clerodendrum bungei   A suckering shrub that grows to 6ft (1.8m) with dark green, very fetid leaves and large flat heads of sweetly scented pink flowers from midsummer onwards. One plant can scent a whole area of the garden. Hardy to 10°F (−12°C), US zones 8–10.

Clerodendrum trichotomum   A large shrub or small tree that grows to 18ft (5.3m) with scented white flowers from red calyces, which then become starry and surround the deep blue berries. The leaves have a slightly fetid scent. Hardy to 10°F (−12°C), US zones 8–10. Native to eastern Asia, with var. *fargesii*, possibly a hardier variety, in western China.

Clerodendrum bungei

Genista

Mount Etna Broom *Genista aetnensis*
A small upright tree that grows to 30ft (9m) with
weeping branches, green twigs but no leaves and
masses of small yellow flowers in late summer. A
native to Sicily and Sardinia, growing on dry hills
and needing well-drained soil and sun in gardens.
Hardy to 10°F (−12°C), US zones 8–10.

PLANTING HELP   Mount Etna Broom will
grow well in poor dry soil, which makes it an
excellent plant for city gardens. It is rather
top-heavy and may need staking, especially if it is
sighted in a windy spot.

Clethra

Sweet Pepper Bush *Clethra alnifolia*
An upright suckering shrub that grows to around
6ft (1.8m) with narrow leaves and spikes of small
creamy flowers in late summer. The scent is
delicate and sweet. There are a few pink-flowered
forms and a large form named 'Paniculata'. A very
hardy shrub to −30°F (−35°C), US zones 4–8.
Those lucky enough to garden in frost-free areas
can grow **Clethra arborea**, the Madeiran Lily-of-
the-valley tree, an evergreen with spikes of
nodding flowers. It will also flower as a bush when
grown in a large pot. Hardy to 32°F (0°C), US
zone 10 or a little less.

PLANTING HELP   *Clethra alnifolia* is happiest
on damp, peaty soils, but will also do well in the
same conditions as suit Rhododendrons.
Clethra arborea needs
similar conditions,
but prefers a slightly
drier position.

Genista aetnensis at Goatchers' Arboretum, Sussex

Sweet Pepper
Bush

Clerodendrum trichotomum at Knightshayes

Lavandula angustifolia 'Rosea'

Lavandula angustifolia 'Imperial Gem'

Lavandula angustifolia 'Beechwood Blue'

Lavender

There are over 30 different species of *Lavandula* native to the Mediterranean, North Africa, Arabia and India, and many cultivated varieties. All are highly aromatic, attractive shrubs; there are few prettier sights than a well-kept lavender hedge in full flower.

English Lavender

PLANTING HELP
Lavenders vary in their hardiness depending on their origins and on the prevailing soil and weather conditions, but they all dislike cold waterlogged soil, so a sunny, well-drained site is essential. To keep lavenders in good shape, trim them back in spring or dead-head after flowering; most will still start to look leggy after a few years and are

LAVENDER

Lavender with grey hedges of *Santolina* in the Herb Garden at Arley Hall in Cheshire

then best replaced. Rooted cuttings are now commercially available, or you can take your own in the autumn. Be ready to protect the less hardy types from severe frost damage in winter with fleece, straw or bracken.

Common or English Lavender *Lavandula angustifolia* This evergreen is native to the Mediterranean area, but is one of the hardiest species, making it popular in gardens in temperate climates; it is also grown commercially for the production of lavender oil. When mature the bush is about 3ft (90cm) high and wide, with aromatic, long, narrow grey green leaves; in June and July it is covered with short spikes of fragrant purplish blue flowers. Hardy to 10°F (−12°C), US zones 8–10 or a little below. There are several varieties of English Lavender, including two white varieties, 'Alba' and the dwarf 'Nana Alba' (*not illustrated here*). Other garden varieties include:

'Beechwood Blue' Grows to about 2ft (60cm), with greyish green leaves and rich blue flowers.

'Munstead' Another variety very suitable for hedging, as it is low-growing, to about 18in (45cm) and bears its purplish blue flowers on short stems.

'Imperial Gem' A fairly low growing compact variety to 24in (60cm), with dark purple flowers.

'Rosea' (syn. 'Munstead Pink', 'Nana Rosea') Grows to 2ft (60cm) and has pale pink flowers.

Lavandula angustifolia 'Munstead'

85

A hedge of 'Papillon' at Odile Mesqualier's, Lyon

Lavandula × intermedia 'Grappenhall'

Lavandula × *intermedia* 'Grappenhall'
Another good choice for cool gardens, as it is nearly as hardy as *L. angustifolia*. It makes a bush to about 2½ft (75cm) tall, with greyish green leaves and spikes of pale bluish mauve flowers held well above the foliage. The whole plant is very strongly scented and it is late flowering (from about early August to October), providing interest long after most other lavenders have finished. Hardy to 10°F (−12°C), US zones 8–10 or a little less. 'Seal' (*not illustrated*) is another good, late flowering variety, similar to 'Grappenhall' but taller with light blue flowers.

Lavandula dentata A spreading but upright bush, this species has particularly well-scented, rather sticky, pale green toothed leaves. It produces its pale blue flowers with conspicuous bracts throughout the year, but is even less hardy than French Lavender (*see below*). Good for a greenhouse in cool climates or for a pot. Hardy to 32°F (0°C), US zone 10.

French Lavender *Lavandula stoechas* This attractive and aromatic evergreen shrub is native to Spain and Portugal and is commonly grown throughout the Mediterranean region. It grows up to about 2ft (60cm) high and has small narrow leaves and spikes of small dark mauve flowers with conspicuous bracts in April–June. It is rather tender in parts of Britain and N Europe, but for short periods only will tolerate temperatures down to about 20°F (−6°C), US zones 9–10. There are a number of forms of French Lavender in cultivation, perhaps the most striking of these being **'Papillon'** (*L. stoechas* subsp. *pedunculata*), with large, bright purple bracts, and the lesser known **'Marshwood'**, which has a similar flower, but in a paler, slightly bluish purple.

Lavandula dentata

Lavandula stoechas 'Papillon'

Lavandula 'Marshwood'

Brugmansia × candida 'Grand Marnier'

Brugmansia × candida 'Knightii'

Daturas

These large-flowered shrubby daturas or *Brugmansia*, as they are now called, are among the most spectacular of all scented plants for the garden. All of them, except the red-flowered *Brugmansia sanguinea* and its yellow variety, have a heady scent which pours out of the huge trumpet flowers towards evening. Hardy to 32°F (0°C), US zone 10.

PLANTING HELP   Daturas will thrive outdoors in a huge pot or tub in a sheltered position, and do well in a shady conservatory. They are very susceptible to frost, but otherwise easy to grow, provided they are given masses of water and fertilizer throughout the summer. Plants grown indoors are prone to attack by red spider mite which may make the leaves go yellow, but this pest is not usually troublesome outside.

***Brugmansia × candida* 'Knightii'** (syn. *Datura* 'Knightii')   A tall shrub that grows to 12ft (3.5m) with huge, white, double hanging flowers and an extra row of petal lobes in the throat.

***Brugmansia* × *candida* 'Grand Marnier'**
A similar shrub which produces single huge flowers of pale apricot yellow.

Passionflower

***Passiflora* 'Incense'** (*P. incarnata* × *P. cincinnata*)
A new American cultivar, raised at the Subtropical Horticulture Research Station in Florida. This variety is very vigorous and flowers prolifically. The fragrant, deep purple flowers, to 5in (12cm) across, are produced throughout the summer and autumn. Fruit edible, egg-shaped, light olive green when ripe. Hardy to 20°F (–6°C), US zones 9–10.

PLANTING HELP   Needs good soil in a warm position with ample summer heat. Can survive temperatures as low as 17°F (–8°C) for short periods if the root is protected. Although the top growth will die off, new shoots will appear from the roots during the summer.

Cestrum

***Cestrum parqui*   A deciduous shrub that grows to 10ft (3m) tall with greenish yellow flowers, 1in (2.5cm) long, fragrant at night. Native to Chile, growing on forest margins and flowering in summer and autumn. Leaves narrow, acrid when bruised. *Cestrum nocturnum*, an evergreen native to the West Indies, has greenish white flowers also strongly scented at night. Hardy to 20°F (–6°C), US zones 9–10.

PLANTING HELP   For any good soil with water in summer. The plant can be treated as an herbaceous perennial, cut down to the ground in winter, with the root protected against frost.

Chilean Jasmine

Mandevilla laxa (syn. *M. suaveolens*)   An often deciduous, fast-growing twining climber that grows to 16ft (4.5m) with cordate leaves and pure white, scented flowers, 3in (8cm) across, the tube 1in (2.5cm) long. In spite of its name it is not native to Chile but to Argentina (Tucuman province) and Bolivia, flowering in summer. Hardy to 20°F (–6°C), US zones 9–10 or a little below.

PLANTING HELP   Easily grown in warm gardens in good soil, with water in summer. It can be trained up wires on a wall, or allowed to scramble through a shrub or small tree.

Passionflower *Passiflora* 'Incense'

Cestrum parqui

Chilean Jasmine *Mandevilla laxa*

Amaryllis belladonna in September at Serre de la Madonne, near Menton, SE France

Amaryllis belladonna

Hedychium coronarium in Malawi

Belladonna

Amaryllis belladonna A large bulb which bears pale pink, sweetly scented flowers around 4in (10cm) across in autumn before the flat leaves appear. A native of the Cape region of South Africa where it flowers especially well after bush fires. Various shades of pink as well as white-flowered clones are in cultivation. Hardy to 20°F (–6°C), US zones 9–10.

PLANTING HELP   Needs good soil with water in winter and spring, dry in summer. In cool areas it is best planted at the foot of a warm wall.

Crinum

Crinum × powellii A huge bulb with a tall tuft of curled leaves to 3½ft (1m) tall and a tall stem with a loose umbel of nodding pink or white flowers, around 5in (12cm) long. A garden hybrid between two South African species and hardier than either. Hardy to 20°F (–6°C), US zones 9–10, provided the bulbs are planted deeply with their tips just below ground.

PLANTING HELP   Easily grown in any soil, given sufficient water and warmth.

Crinum × powellii growing in an open garden in east Kent

Hedychium

Hedychiums are tall, leafy, ginger-like plants, easily grown in a conservatory, or in mild climates outdoors in a moist sheltered border. The flowers are deliciously scented, so are ideal to cut and bring in to the house, where they will last for several days.

PLANTING HELP   Needs good rich soil with ample water in summer, drier in winter.

Ginger Lily *Hedychium gardnerianum*
A very fine and easily grown tall perennial with stiff stems to 6ft (1.8m), ending in heads 10–16in (25–40cm) long, with many well-scented lemon yellow flowers. A native of India, growing in wet forests in the Himalayas. Hardy to 20°F (–6°C), US zones 9–10, provided the rhizomes are protected from freezing.

Hedychium coronarium   The short flower heads produce a succession of wonderfully scented white flowers 2in (5cm) wide. Native from India to Indonesia, growing in damp places and by streams in the forest. Hardy to 40°F (5°C), US zone 11 or a little below; alternatively dig up the rhizomes and bring them indoors for the winter.

Ginger Lily in a cold greenhouse

Elaeagnus macrophylla

Elaeagnus × ebbingii

A young tree of *Cercidiphyllum japonicum* in Devon

Buddleja

Buddleja auriculata
A lax arching shrub that grows to 10ft (3m) with thin leaves and a large branching inflorescence of small but spice-scented, creamy white flowers, ¼in (0.5cm) across, the tube ⅓in (8mm), fading orange. Hardy to 20°F (−6°C), US zones 9–10.

PLANTING HELP   Often grown on a wall for its autumn scent, but good in the greenhouse too, where it will continue to flower throughout the winter.

Buddleja auriculata

Elaeagnus

The evergreen members of this genus are terrific evergreen hedging or specimen plants, useful in the garden and much prized for the delicious scent of their autumn flowers. You will often notice the scent and find it difficult to see where it is coming from, as the small whitish flowers are hidden by the leaves.

PLANTING HELP   These evergreen *Elaeagnus* grow in any good soil, with water in summer. They are especially useful for growing by the sea as they are very tolerant of salt.

Elaeagnus macrophylla   A spreading or scrambling evergreen shrub that grows to 6ft (1.8m) or more, with leaves shiny dark green above, silvery beneath, to 2½in (6cm) long. Flowers formed in October and November, small but very sweetly scented on warm days. Hardy to 10°F (−12°C), US zones 8–10.

Elaeagnus × ebbingii   A hybrid between *E. macrophylla* and *E. pungens*, with slightly larger leaves than either parent and tougher than

E. macrophylla. Hardy to 10°F (−12°C), US zones 8–10 or a little below. A creamy-edged form 'Gilt Edge' is commonly cultivated, as is the yellow-centred 'Limelight'.

Cercidiphyllum

Cercidiphyllum japonicum Katsura Tree   This lovely tree has a unique smell of burning sugar in autumn; the scent is carried on the air, so you often notice it before you see the tree. In addition to this, *Cercidiphyllum japonicum* is one of the best small trees to plant in a cool area. It is reasonably fast-growing, hardy and very graceful. It is also one of the first trees to colour in autumn and the new leaves are a delightful purplish pink. Hardy to −10°F (−23°C), US zones 6–9.

PLANTING HELP   Easily grown in any good, moist peaty or leafy soil. Best in shelter and partial shade when young.

Witch-hazel

Hamamelis virginiana   Although the Asiatic species of Witch-hazel flowers in late winter or spring, this American species flowers in the autumn, at the same time as its leaves colour. It is found all down the eastern seaboard growing in moist woods and by lakes from Nova Scotia to Florida. Flowers smaller than *H. mollis*, but with a sweet, spicy smell. Hardy to −20°F (−29°C), US zones 5–9. It is from the leaves and twigs of this Witch-hazel that the lotion is made.

PLANTING HELP   Easily grown in any good, moist peaty or leafy soil. Best in partial shade.

Mahonia

Mahonia × media   The excellent varieties of *Mahonia × media* usually flower before Christmas. With their bold spiny leaves and long spikes around 9in (23cm) of small yellow flowers, they are one of the most striking hardy shrubs. The stems are upright when young, soon reaching 10ft (3m) and without pruning eventually grow very large. Hardy to 10°F (−12°C), US zones 8–10 or a little below. **'Charity'** is one of the most popular of this group. Its parentage is *M. lomariifolia*, upright with particularly stiff, spiky leaves, crossed with *M. japonica*, the species with the best scent of all, but rather hidden flowers.

PLANTING HELP
Easily grown in any good, leafy soil. Best in partial shade.

Witch-hazel

Mahonia × media 'Charity', the original plant in the Savill garden, Windsor

Index

INDEX

INDEX